SPECTRUM®

Sight Words

Grade 1

Spectrum®
An imprint of Carson-Dellosa Publishing LLC
P.O. Box 35665
Greensboro, NC 27425 USA

ISBN 978-1-4838-1189-5

02-227147811

Table of Contents

Notes to Parents and Teachers 4

Sight Word Vocabulary

am, big, box 5
ran, let, got 6
play, ball, hat 8
call, jump, sat 9
red, black, yellow, green 11
white, blue, brown, color 12
say, ask, friend 14
way, may, today 15
girl, look, find 17
dog, run, sit, yes 18
four, five, six, seven, eight 20
nine, ten, money, buy 21
under, upon, next, near 23
high, tree, found 24
until, into, same 26
hard, part, round 27
fat, funny, might 29
saw, only, such, never 30
live, house, home 32
mother, sister, brother 33
each, own, name 35
year, also, fall 36
sleep, morning, night, bed 38
o'clock, early, school 39
open, close, leave 41
off, door, don't 42
read, book, over 44
another, because 45
car, far, ride, around 47
back, away, town, took 48
every, anything, think 50
people, could, too 51
men, woman, along 53
stop, both, walk 54
clean, wash, water 56
carry, hot, warm 57
clothes, coat, cold 59
kind, dress, better 60
please, tell, once 62

Table of Contents

use, made. 63
fly, fast, goes 65
try, though, why 66
food, ate, full. 68
most, more, always. 69
write, letter, dear, love 71
yesterday, soon, fine 73
cut, grow, longer, keep. 75
want, than, should. 76
these, thing, while 78
which, set 79
first, second, third. 81
last, order, stand. 82
where, does, those 84
now, seem, shall 85
eyes, ear, hear 87
face, hand, head 88
fire, sure, start. 90
hold, show, hope. 91
right, left, myself. 93
help, small, pair 94
came, gave, pretty 96
present, bring, sing. 97
happy, wish, thank 99
didn't, end, best 100

Sight Word Cloze Sentences 102

Sight Word Scrambled Sentences 112

Sight Word Flash Cards 117

Fry Instant Sight Word Lists. 145

Answer Key 148

Notes to Parents and Teachers

Whenever a young child reads, 50 to 75% of the words he or she comes across are from the Fry Instant Sight Word List. This is a highly respected, research-based list of the 300 most frequently used words in the English language. Typically, these high-frequency words do not follow regular phonics patterns or spelling rules, making them very difficult for young children to sound out or decode. Consequently, learning to recognize these words immediately "by sight" is a critical first step to successful, confident, fluent reading.

Spectrum Sight Words for First Grade, and its companion, *Spectrum Sight Words for Kindergarten*, introduce, practice, and review all of the words on this list to help children develop sight word mastery, confidence, and fluency as they encounter these words in both reading and writing. *Spectrum Sight Words* are intended for use in school programs or at home with 5-, 6-, and 7-year-olds. The contents are also suitable for older children needing more practice, or for younger children developing early reading skills.

Follow these helpful steps when using this book:
- Follow the exact sequence of the book's exercises, as each sight word is introduced—and then reviewed—in its specific order on the Fry Instant Sight Word List, beginning with the most frequently appearing words.
- Encourage your child to work at his or her own pace, and offer support and praise as he or she completes the exercises.
- Use the sight word flash card pages at the back of the book to create a set of flash cards for practice in reading and writing the sight words.
- Take advantage of the blank flash cards to personalize your child's flash card set.
- Review and evaluate sight word memory by having your child use the sight words in context, using the cloze sentence activities.
- Help your child develop and demonstrate sentence sense by using the scrambled sentence activities to reorganize sight words in correct sentence order.

As teachers and parents, it is our goal to support and foster the learning of all of our children. Activities and materials in *Spectrum Sight Words for First Grade* help meet those needs by promoting the appropriate pacing and challenge that allows each child to master reading success.

Target words: **am, big, box**

Directions: Write the words below. Say them as you write them.

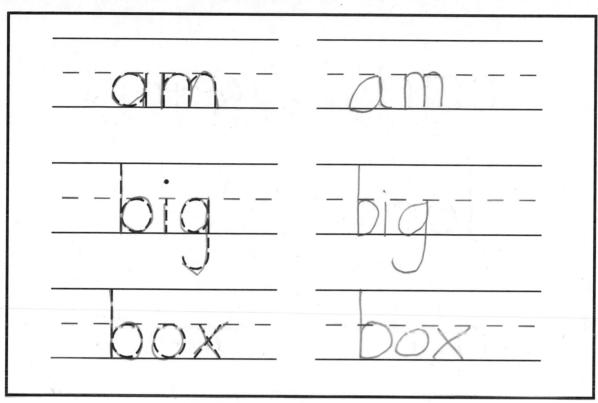

am   am

big   big

box   box

Directions: Write the missing word in each sentence.

1. I ___am___ good at playing with my dog.

2. My dog is ___big___.

3. He is in a ___box___.

Now, write a sentence with these words in it: **big   box**

I got a big box of toys for my birthday.

Target words: **ran, let, got**

Directions: Write the words below. Say them as you write them.

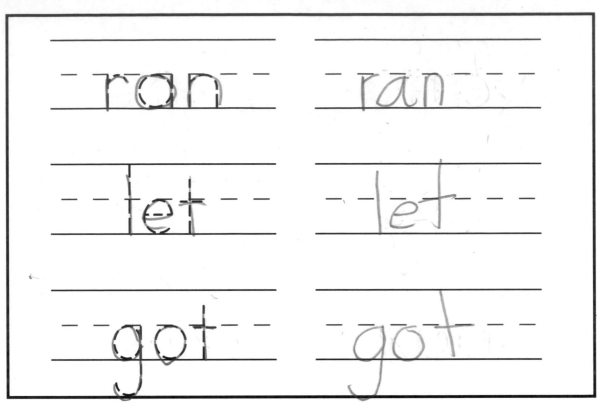

ran   ran

let   let

got   got

Directions: Write the missing word in each sentence.

1. I ____got____ a dog.

2. He ____ran____ in the yard.

3. I ____let____ him lick me.

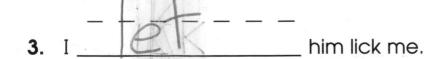

Now, write a sentence with these words in it: **dog got**

I got up early to feed the dog

Target words: **am, big, box, ran, let, got**

Directions: Find and circle the words from the box. Words can go →
or ↓.

| ~~am~~ |
| **big** |
| **box** |
| ~~ran~~ |
| **let** |
| **got** |

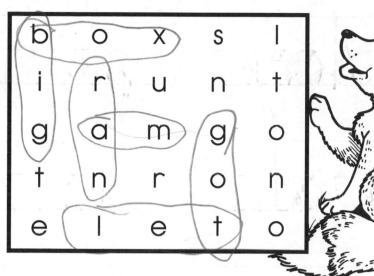

b	o	x	s	l
i	r	u	n	t
g	a	m	g	o
t	n	r	o	n
e	l	e	t	o

Directions: Draw a line to connect the words that rhyme.

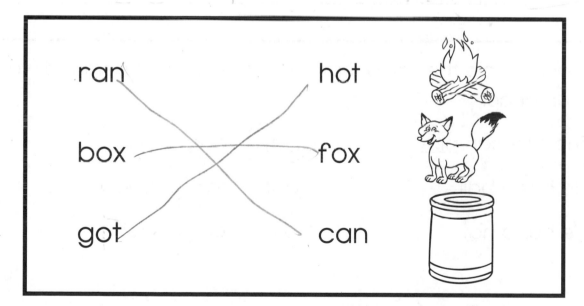

ran   hot

box   fox

got   can

Target words: play, ball, hat

Directions: Write the words below. Say them as you write them.

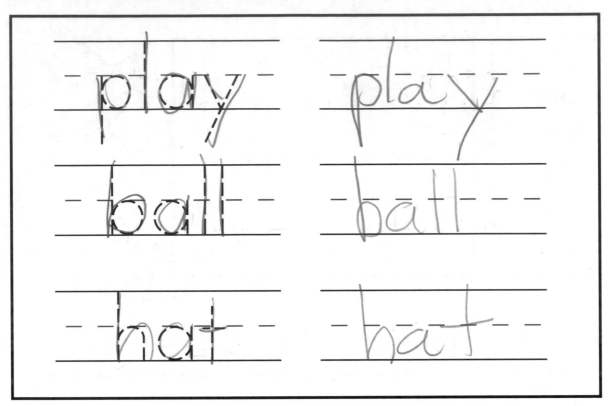

Directions: Circle the word that rhymes with the underlined word in each sentence.

1. The boy can <u>play</u>.   (day)   dog   pup

2. He has a <u>ball</u>.   bat   (tall)   bug

3. He has a <u>hat</u>.   hot   (bat)   ball

Target words: **call, jump, sat**

Directions: Write the words below. Say them as you write them.

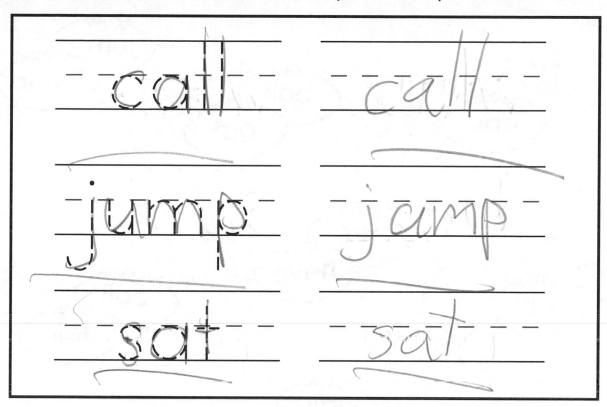

Directions: Write the missing word in each sentence.

1. The frog can ___*jump*___ .

2. He ___*sat*___ by the pond.

3. I will not ___*call*___ to him.

4. ___*paul*___ rhymes with **ball**.

Target words: play, ball, hat, call, jump, sat

Directions: Circle each set of footballs that have rhyming words on them.

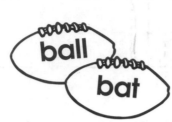

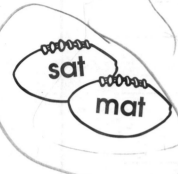

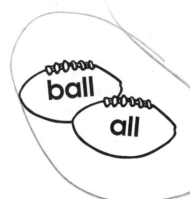

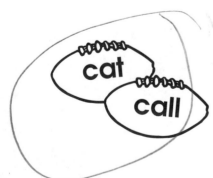

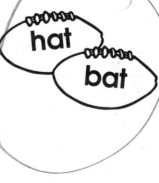

Target words: **red, black, yellow, green**

Directions: Write the words below. Say them as you write them.

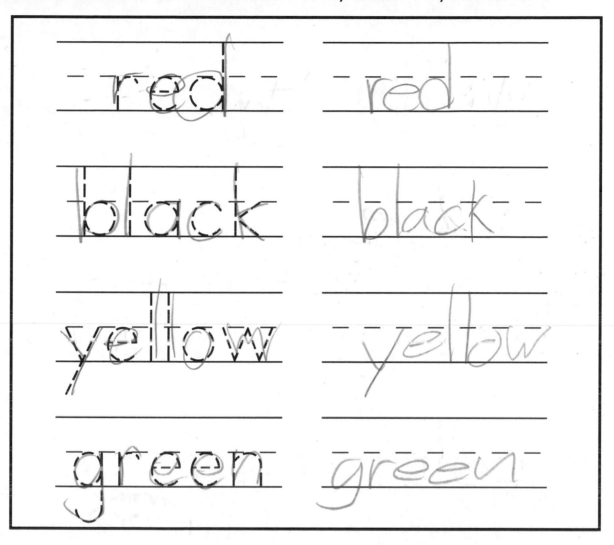

red red

black black

yellow yellow

green green

Directions: Write the missing word in each sentence.

1. A bear is __black__.

2. An apple is __red__.

Target words: white, blue, brown, color

Directions: Write the words below. Say them as you write them.

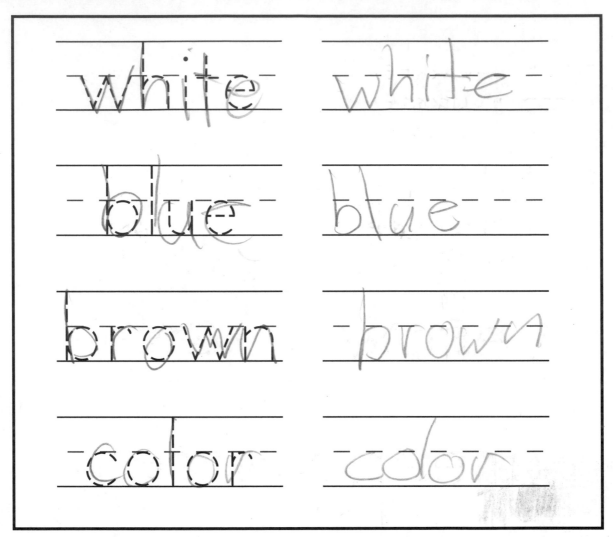

white   white

blue   blue

brown   brown

color   color

Directions: Write the missing word in each sentence.

white   blue   (brown)   color

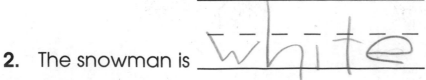

1. I can color the bear _brown_.

2. The snowman is _white_.

Target words: red, black, yellow, green, white, blue, brown, color

Directions:

1. Color bear number 1 blue.
2. Color bear number 2 green.
3. Color bear number 3 brown.
4. Color bear number 4 yellow.
5. Color bear number 5 white.
6. Color bear number 6 black.
7. Color bear number 7 red.

Target words: say, ask, friend

Directions: Write the words below. Say them as you write them.

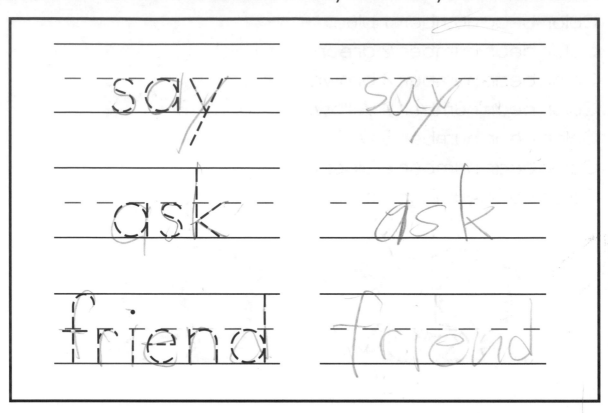

Directions: The words **say, ask,** and **friend** are hiding in the lines below. Find and circle them. Now, color the boxes.

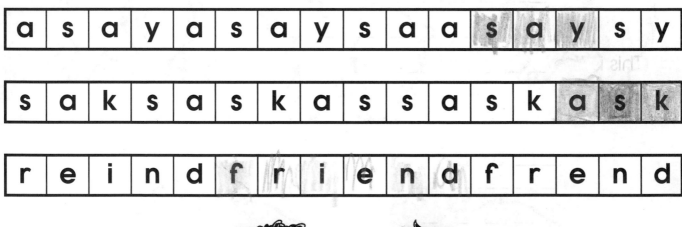

| a | s | a | y | a | s | a | y | s | a | a | s | a | y | s | y |

| s | a | k | s | a | s | k | a | s | s | a | s | k | a | s | k |

| r | e | i | n | d | f | r | i | e | n | d | f | r | e | n | d |

Hi, how are you?

I'm fine. How are you?

Target words: **way, may, today**

Directions: Write the words below. Say them as you write them.

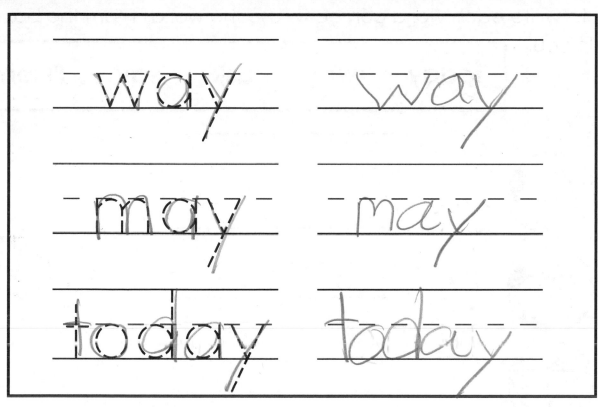

Directions: Write the missing word in each sentence. Now, circle the words in each sentence that rhyme.

1. This is the _way_ I want to play.

2. _Today_ I say this?

3. _May_ is Monday.

Directions: Write 3 more words that rhyme with **way** and **may**.

Pay   play   _____

Target words: say, ask, friend, way, may, today

Directions: The letters in the words are mixed up. Unscramble them to write each word correctly. Use the words from the box to help you.

today	way	ask	say	friend

 1. ksa   *ask*

 2. yas   *say*

 3. drfeni   *friend*

 4. doayt   *today*

 5. wya   *way*

Directions: Unscramble the words in this sentence. Now, write the sentence.

I play with my drfeni.

I Play with my friend

Target words: girl, look, find

Directions: Write the words below. Say them as you write them.

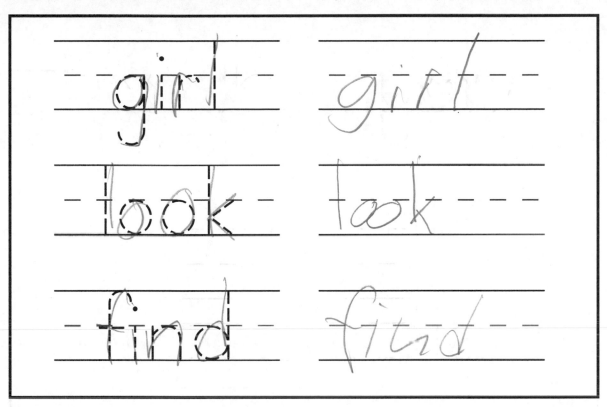

Directions:

1. Circle the box that says **look**.
2. Color the box that says **find**.
3. Put an **X** on the box that says **girl**.

 girl

like

 find

fun

 look

 boy

Directions: Circle the two words in each row that are the same.

love	look	like	look
find	four	five	find
girl	girl	got	goat

Target words: dog, run, sit, yes

Directions: Write the words below. Say them as you write them.

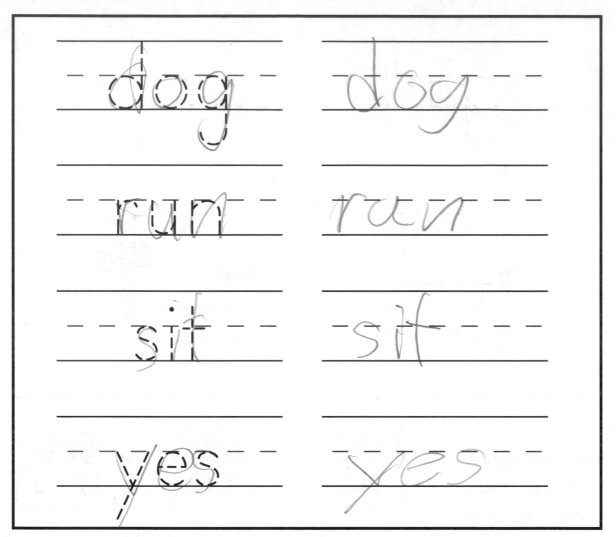

Directions: Find and circle the dog bones with the words from the box on them.

| dog | run | sit | yes |

yes

ran   dog   yet

set   run   day   sit

How many did you circle? _____

NAME _____

Target words: girl, look, find, dog, run, sit, yes

Directions: Use the words from the box to write the missing word in each sentence.

| girl | look | find | dog | run | sit | yes |

1. A _____girl_____ had a dog.

2. He liked to _____ray_____ fast.

3. One day she lost her _____dog_____ .

4. She could not _____find_____ him.

5. She had to _____look_____ for him. Did she find him?

6. _____ys_____ , she did.

7. Now she wants him to _____.

Spectrum Sight Words
Grade 1

Sight Word Vocabulary

19

Target words: four, five, six, seven, eight

Directions: Write the words below. Say them as you write them.

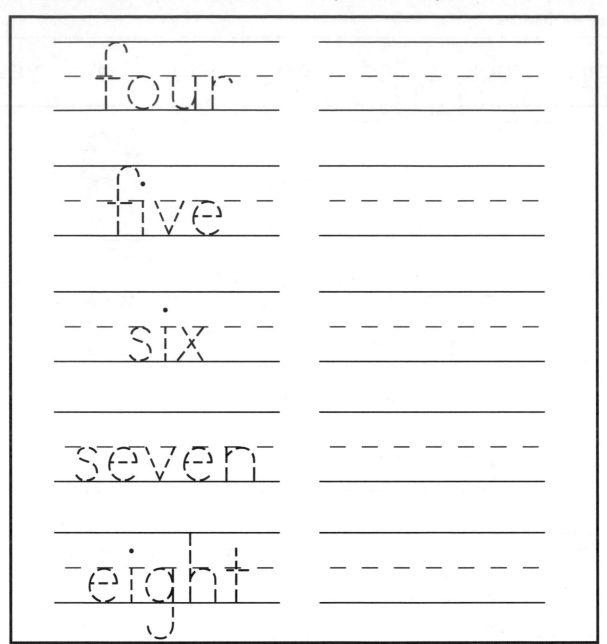

Directions: Draw a line to the number that matches the word.

six	4
four	8
five	6
seven	5
eight	7

Target words: **nine, ten, money, buy**

Directions: Write the words below. Say them as you write them.

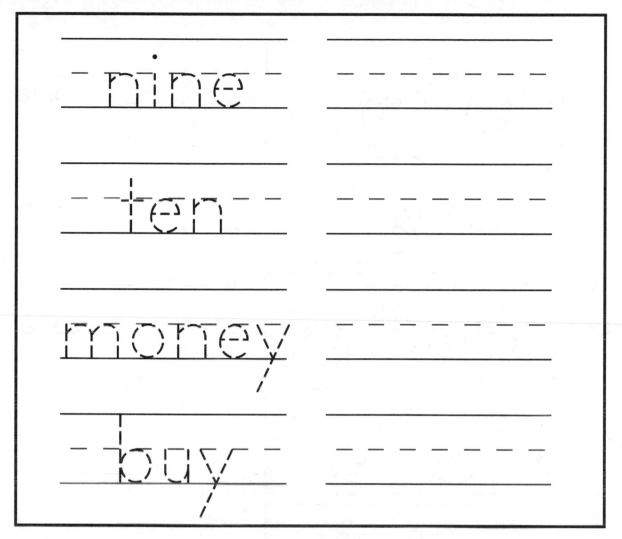

Directions: Write the missing word in each sentence. Then, write the answers.

_____

1. Can she _____ a pencil?

2. How much _____ does she have?

Target words: four, five, six, seven, eight, nine, ten, money, buy

Directions: Draw a line from each box to the word that tells how many coins there are.

nine

five

seven

four

eight

ten

six

Sight Word Vocabulary

Target words: **under, upon, next, near**

Directions: Write the words below. Say them as you write them.

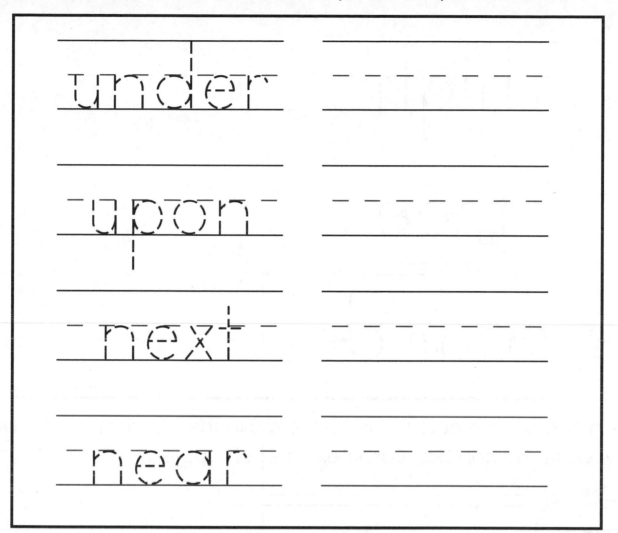

under

upon

next

near

Directions: Write the missing word in each sentence.

1. The rock is _____ a tree.

2. The frog sits _____ a lily pad.

3. The mouse is _____ to the elephant.

Target words: high, tree, found

Directions: Write the words below. Say them as you write them.

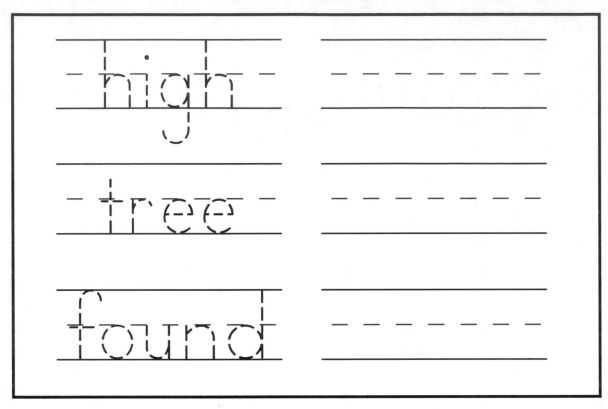

Directions: Unscramble the letters to make the words from the box.
Now, write the correct word next to each apple.

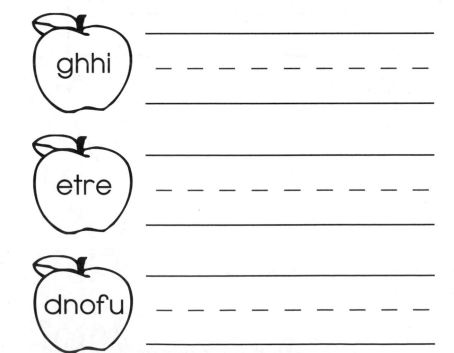

Target words: under, upon, next, near, high, tree, found

Directions: Read each sentence. Now, write it on the line.

The boy ran next to his dog.

_____

- -

_____

They sat upon a bench.

_____

- -

_____

A rock is under the tree.

_____

- -

_____

He threw it high up.

_____

- -

_____

He found it near the tree.

_____

- -

_____

Target words: until, into, same

Directions: Write the words below. Say them as you write them.

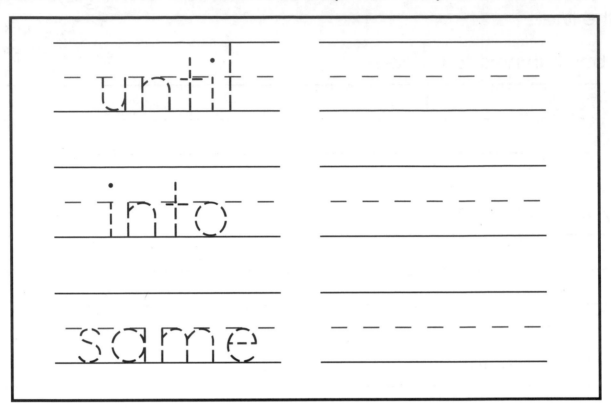

Directions: Color the apples that have the same words on them.

Target words: **hard, part, round**

Directions: Write the words below. Say them as you write them.

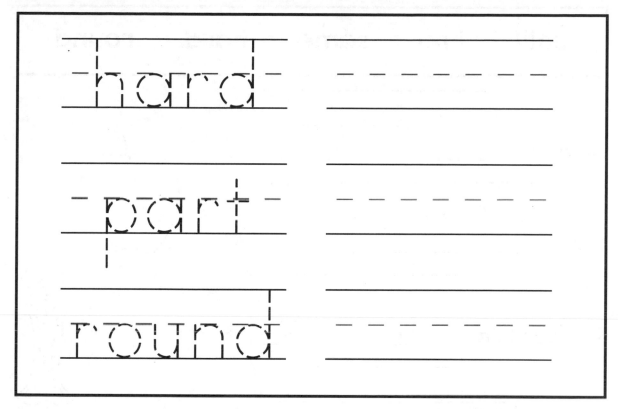

Directions: Draw a line to connect the bouncing balls to get to the basket. Use the words from the box.

round	hard
part	

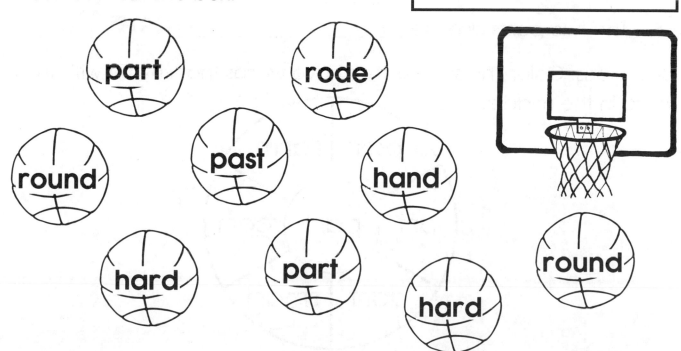

Target words: **until, into, same, hard, part, round**

Directions: Write the missing word in each sentence.

until	into	same	hard	round

_____

– – – – – –

1. An apple is _____.

_____

– – – – – – –

2. It is _____.

_____

– – – – – – – –

3. You can bite _____ it.

_____

– – – – – – –

4. Eat it all _____ it is gone.

_____

– – – – – – – –

5. The two parts are the _____.

Directions: Color the spaces that have words that rhyme with the word in the middle.

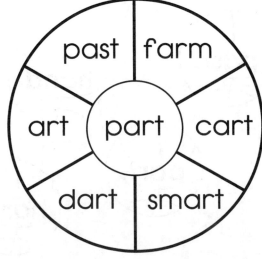

Target words: fat, funny, might

Directions: Write the words below. Say them as you write them.

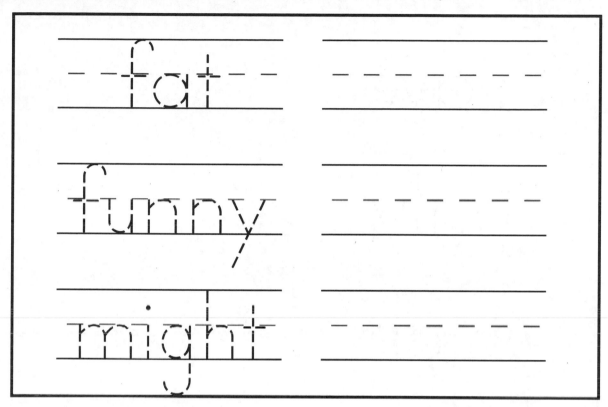

Directions: Draw a line to connect the words that rhyme.

fat   night

funny   bunny

might   cat

Now, draw a
fat, funny mouse.

Target words: **saw, only, such, never**

Directions: Write the words below. Say them as you write them.

Directions: The words **saw, only, such,** and **never** are hiding in the boxes below. Find them and color the boxes that have these words in them.

one	only	on	only
saw	was	sun	saw
much	such	such	more
never	ever	never	even

Target words: fat, funny, might, saw, only, such, never

Directions: Find and circle the words from the box. Words can go →
or ↓.

fat
funny
might
saw
only
such
never

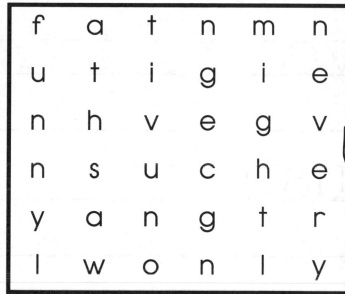

f	a	t	n	m	n
u	t	i	g	i	e
n	h	v	e	g	v
n	s	u	c	h	e
y	a	n	g	t	r
l	w	o	n	l	y

Directions: Color the spaces that have words that rhyme with the
word in the middle of the circle.

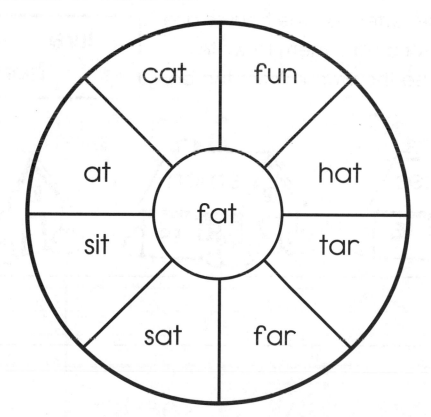

fat

cat, fun, at, hat, fat, sit, tar, sat, far

Target words: **live, house, home**

Directions: Write the words below. Say them as you write them.

Directions: The letters on the houses are mixed up. Unscramble them to write each word. Use the words from the box to help you.

live	house
home	

ohues

emoh

evil

Target words: mother, sister, brother

Directions: Write the words below. Say them as you write them.

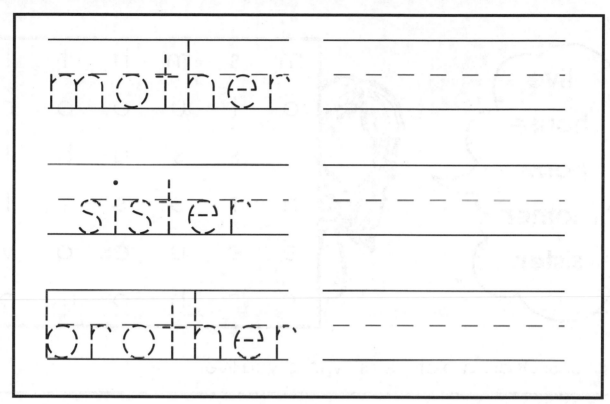

Directions: Select the word from the box that answers these riddles.

| mother | sister | brother |

I am a girl.   _ _ _ _ _ _ _ _ _
                _____

I am a boy.   _ _ _ _ _ _ _ _ _
                _____

I am a woman.   _ _ _ _ _ _ _ _ _
                _____

Now, draw a picture of yourself.

Target words: live, house, home, mother, sister

Directions: Find and circle the words from the box. Words can go ➔ or ↓.

live
house
home
mother
sister

m	s	m	h	t	l
o	i	u	o	e	r
t	s	s	u	h	l
h	t	o	s	t	i
e	e	u	e	o	v
r	r	h	o	m	e

Directions: Draw a picture of where you live.

NAME _____

Target words: each, own, name

Directions: Write the words below. Say them as you write them.

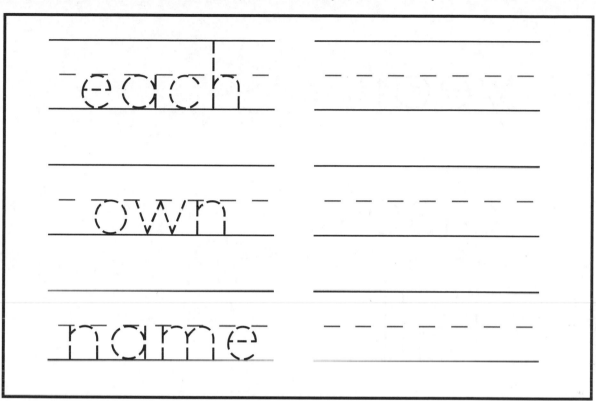

Directions: Read the sentences below and follow the directions.

1. Write your own name on each tag.
2. Color each present blue.
3. What do you think is in the boxes?

_____

– –

_____

Target words: **year, also, fall**

Directions: Write the words below. Say them as you write them.

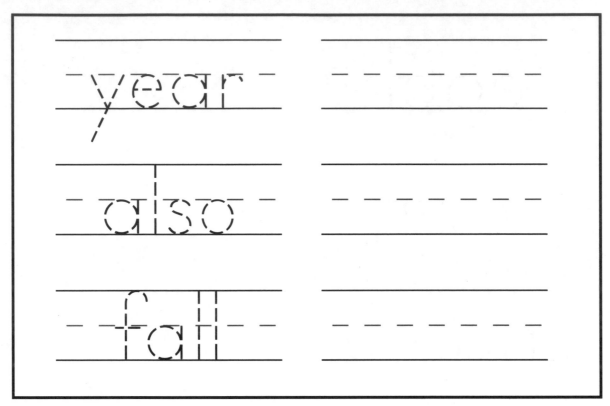

Directions: Read these sentences and draw a picture of them.

Every year the leaves fall.

I like to rake the leaves.

And I also like to jump in them.

Target words: each, own, name, year, also, fall

| each | own | name | year | also | fall |

Directions: Find the leaves that have the words from the box on them. Color them these colors:

each = red   **own** = green   **name** = yellow
year = orange   **also** = brown

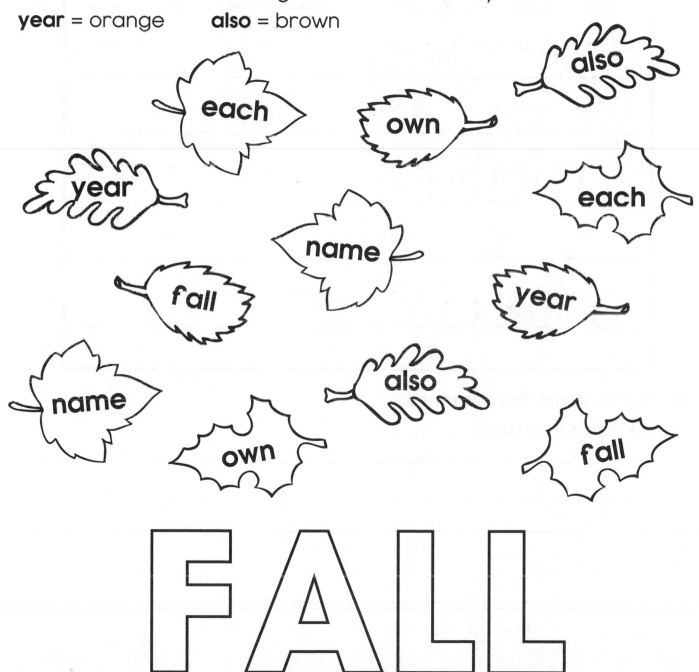

FALL

Target words: sleep, morning, night, bed

Directions: Write the words below. Say them as you write them.

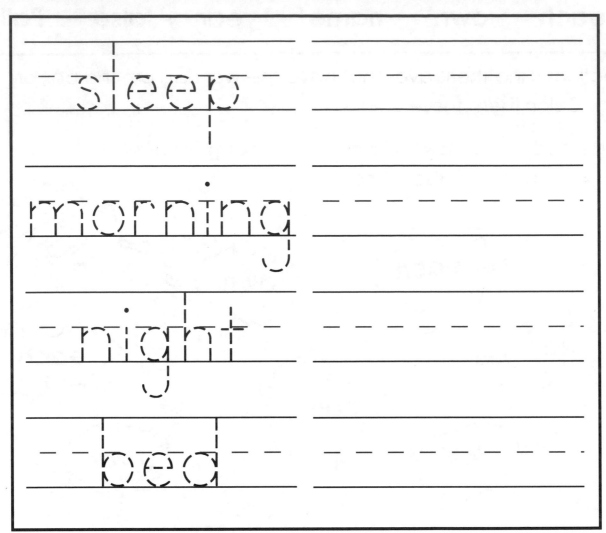

Directions: Write this sentence.

Do you sleep in a bed?

_____

- -

_____

Target words: o'clock, early, school

Directions: Write the words below. Say them as you write them.

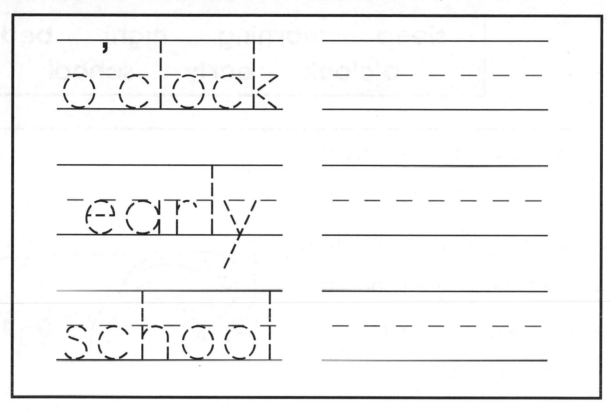

Directions: Read the sentences and follow the directions.

1. Write **one** under the star with the word **o'clock** on it.
2. Write **two** under the star with the word **school** on it.
3. Write **three** under the star with the word **early** on it.

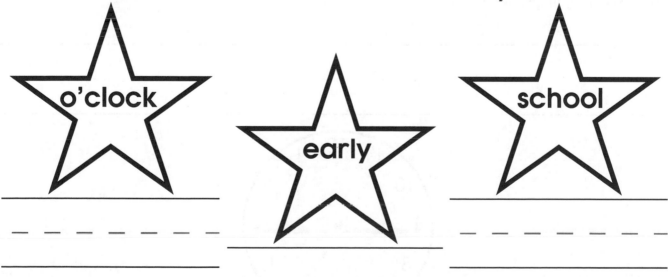

Target words: sleep, morning, night, bed, o'clock, early, school

Directions: Read the story. Now, find and circle the words that are in the box.

sleep	morning	night	bed
	o'clock	early	school

I have to go to bed at eight o'clock at night. I do not like to go to sleep too early. In the morning, I have to get up. When I get up, my dog is there. He wants to go on a walk. So I walk with him before I go to school.

What time do you go to bed? Show it on the clock and write the time on the line.

_____

- - - - - - - - - - - - - - - - - - -

_____

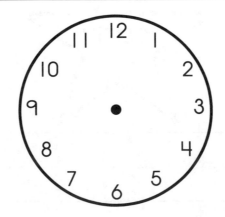

Target words: open, close, leave

Directions: Write the words below. Say them as you write them.

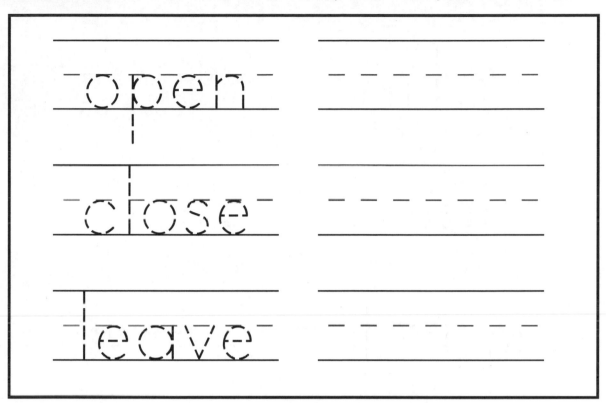

Directions: Draw a picture of each sentence.

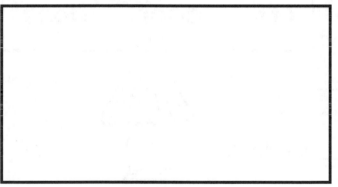

I open the book.

I close the book.

I will leave the book on my bed.

Target words: off, door, don't

Directions: Write the words below. Say them as you write them.

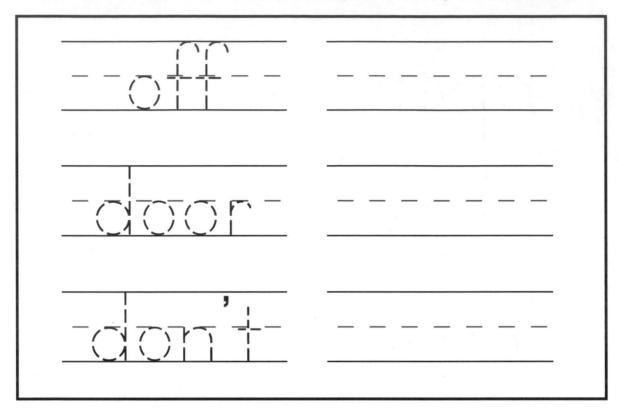

Directions: Write the missing word in each sentence. Use the words from the box to help you.

off	door	don't

_____
_ _ _ _ _ _ _

1. I will turn _____ the light.

_____
_ _ _ _ _ _ _

2. _____ close the door.

_____
_ _ _ _ _ _ _

3. The _____ is open.

Target words: open, close, leave, off, door, don't

Directions: Read the story.
Now, find and circle the
words from the box.

open	close	leave
off	door	don't

One night I had to leave the door

open. I do not like the dark, so I said, "Mom,

don't close the door." Then I said, "Don't

turn the light off." Then I went to sleep.

Directions: Draw a line to connect words that are opposites.

on

open

do

don't

off

close

Target words: read, book, over

Directions: Write the words below. Say them as you write them.

Directions: Several words below are mixed up. Unscramble the letters and write all the words on the lines. Use the words from the box.

book	**over**	**read**	**and**	**can**	**I**	**a**

I _____ nac _____ daer _____ a _____ kobo _____

_____ voer _____ dna _____ voer. _____

Target words: another, because

Directions: Write the words below. Say them as you write them.

another

because

Directions: Draw a picture for each sentence.

I want another dog.

I am hot because the sun is out.

Let's get another pumpkin.

I am cold because I lost my shoes.

Spectrum Sight Words
Grade 1

Sight Word Vocabulary

45

Target words: read, book, over, another, because

Directions: Use the words from the box to complete the story.

read	book	over
another		because

_____

- - - - - - - - - -

The girl is sitting in a chair. She likes to _____

_____

- - - - - - - - - -

her _____ here. She will even

_____

- - - - - - - - - -

read _____ book, too. She has lots of books

_____

- - - - - - - - - -

_____ she likes to read. She will read her

_____

- - - - - - - - - -

books _____ again.

Directions: Circle the books with the same words on them.

Sight Word Vocabulary

NAME _____

Target words: car, far, ride, around

Directions: Write the words below. Say them as you write them.

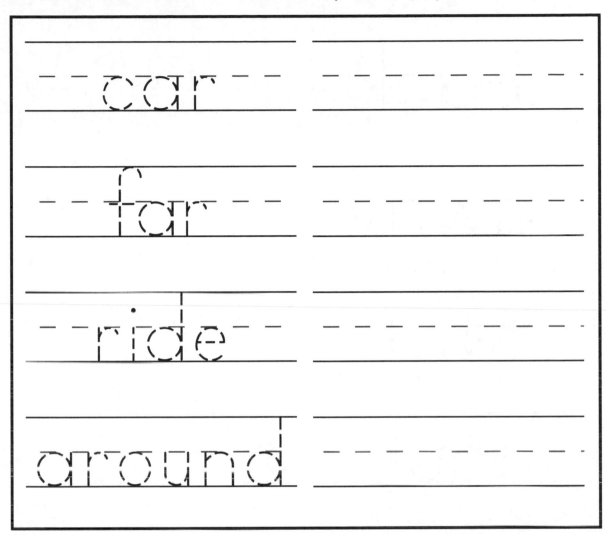

Directions: Color the cars that have words that rhyme with **ride**.

Target words: **back, away, town, took**

Directions: Write the words below. Say them as you write them.

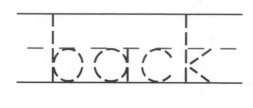 

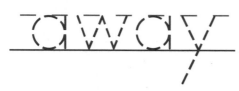 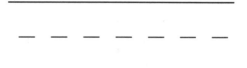

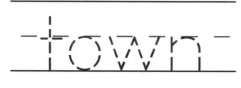 

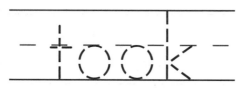

Directions: Read each sentence. Circle the word that rhymes with the underlined word.

1. The car went <u>back</u> home.   bag   sack   come

2. Will the bug go <u>away</u>?   rug   till   stay

3. We went all over <u>town</u>.   too   down   ball

4. It took a <u>long</u> time to get home.   lot   look   song

Target words: car, far, ride, around, back, away, town, took

Directions: Find and circle the words from the box. Words can go →
or ↓.

car
far ride
around back
away town
took

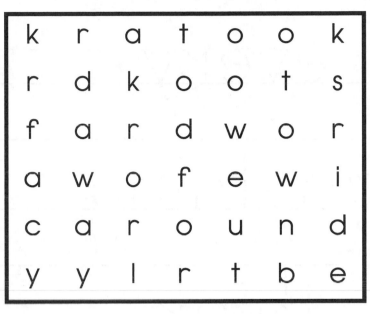

k	r	a	t	o	o	k
r	d	k	o	o	t	s
f	a	r	d	w	o	r
a	w	o	f	e	w	i
c	a	r	o	u	n	d
y	y	l	r	t	b	e

Directions: The words **town** and **ride** are hiding in the boxes below.
Find and circle them.

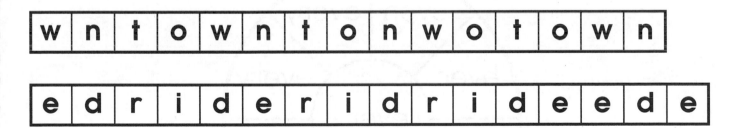

| w | n | t | o | w | n | t | o | n | w | o | t | o | w | n |

| e | d | r | i | d | e | r | i | d | r | i | d | e | e | d | e |

Target words: **every, anything, think**

Directions: Write the words below. Say them as you write them.

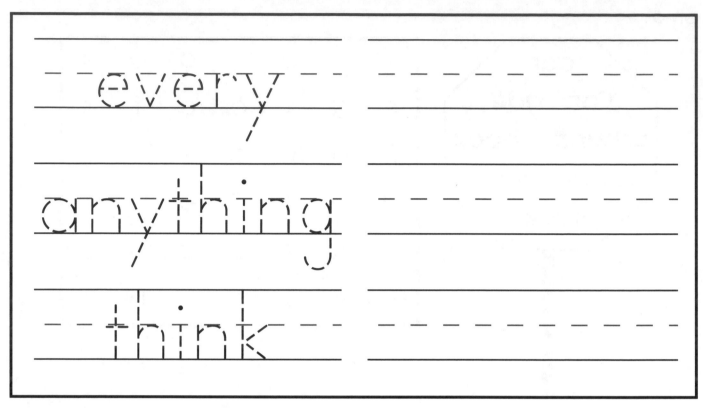

Directions: Color the spaces that have the same word as the one in the middle of the circle.

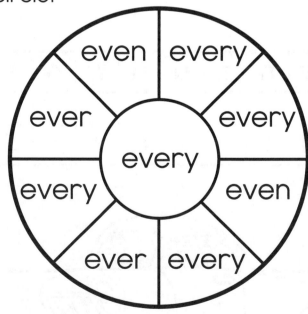

How many spaces did you color? _____

Target words: **people, could, too**

Directions: Write the words below. Say them as you write them.

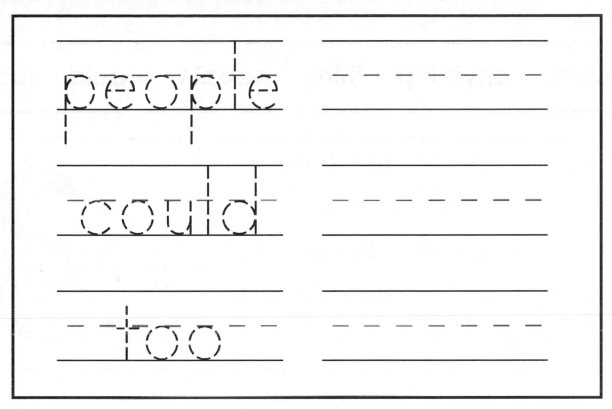

Directions: Unscramble the letters to make the words from the box.
Now, write them on the line under each book.

| could | people | too |

oto   eopple   dcluo

Now, write this sentence.
People could read too.

Target words: **every, anything, think, people, could, too**

Directions: Read the story. Now, find and circle the words from the box.

every	anything	think	people	could	too

I love to read every book I can.

I tell my friends that they could, too.

They could read as many books as I do.

I think lots of people could read anything

they want. Let's read!

Now, write a sentence telling what you think people would like to read about.

_____

_____

_____

_____

_____

Target words: men, woman, along

Directions: Write the words below. Say them as you write them.

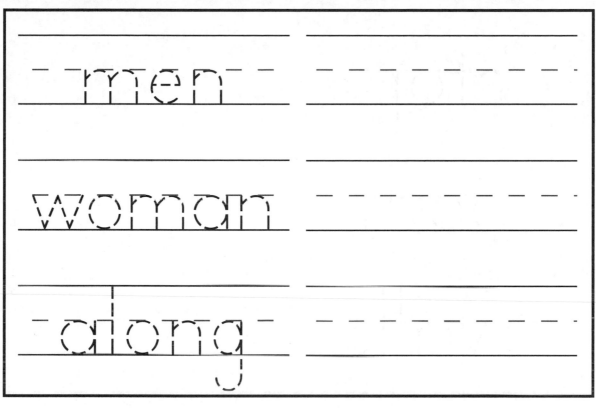

Directions: Color the spaces that have the same word as the one in the middle of the circle.

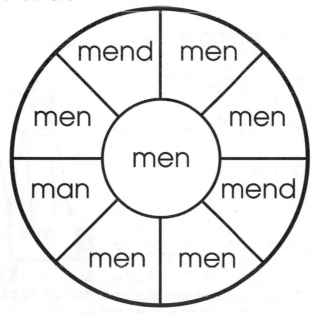

How many spaces did you color? _____

Target words: **stop, both, walk**

Directions: Write the words below. Say them as you write them.

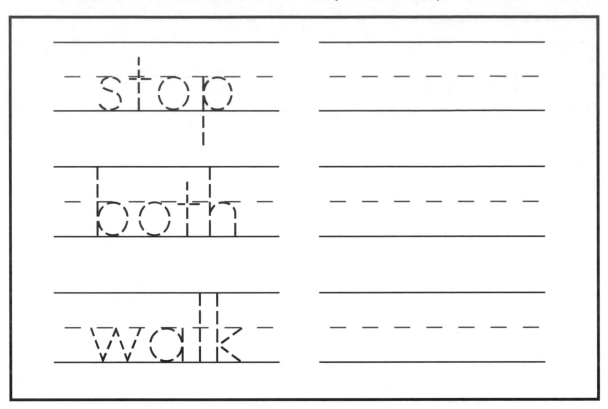

Directions: Look at the picture. Which sentence tells about the picture? Put an **X** by that sentence.

1. _____ Both men are driving a car.

2. _____ Both men will stop eating.

3. _____ Both men walk by the stop sign.

4. _____ The men both jump.

Target words: **men, woman, along, stop, both, walk**

Directions: To get to the street, draw a line to connect the stop signs that contain the words from the box. The first one is done for you.

| men | woman | along | stop | both | walk |

talk   both —— woman   top

women   man   stop   alone

walk   along   men   ball

25

Target words: clean, wash, water

Directions: Write the words below. Say them as you write them.

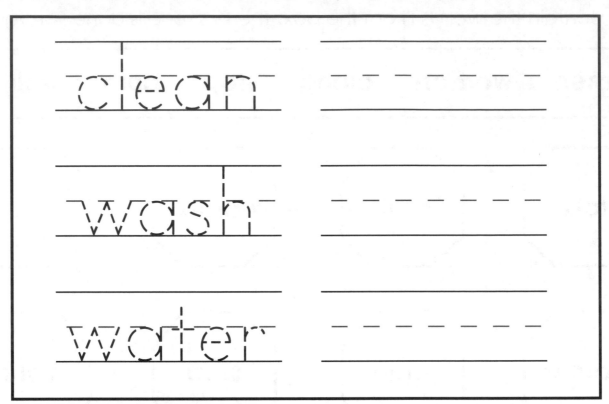

Directions: Unscramble the words on the wash tubs. Now, write each word on the line. Use the words from the box to help you.

swha   retwa   enacl

_____ _____ _____

– – – – – – –   – – – – – – –   – – – – – – –

Now, write this sentence.

Wash with clean water.

_____

– – – – – – – – – – – – – – – – – – – –

Target words: **carry, hot, warm**

Directions: Write the words below. Say them as you write them.

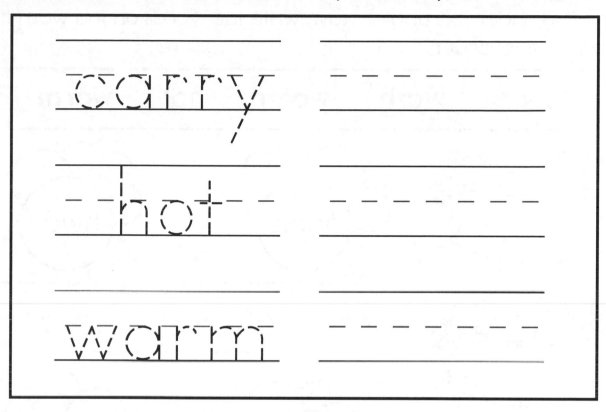

Directions: Draw a line from each bucket to its matching word.

carrot   carry   cart   carry

hot   hop   lot   hot

wash   what   water   water

Target words: clean, wash, water, hot, warm

Directions: Unscramble the words from the box. Write each word on the line under its bubble. Now, write the words on the wash tubs in alphabetical order.

| clean | wash | water | hot | warm |

naelc

_____

hwas

_____

rweat

_____

toh

_____

awrm

_____

Target words: clothes, coat, cold

Directions: Write the words below. Say them as you write them.

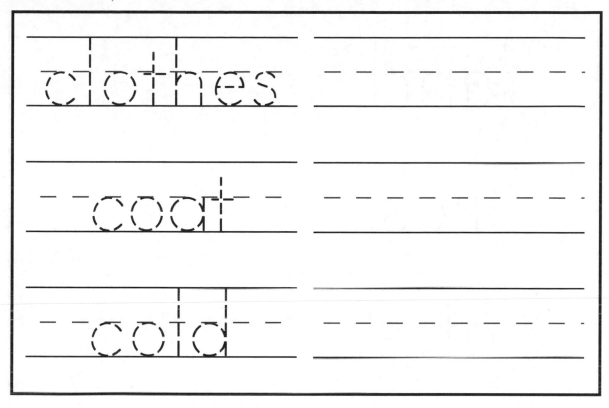

Directions: Color the spaces that have words that rhyme with the same word in the middle of the circle.

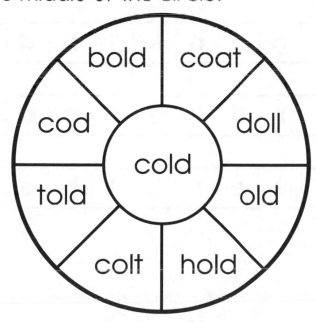

How many spaces did you color? _____

Target words: **kind, dress, better**

Directions: Write the words below. Say them as you write them.

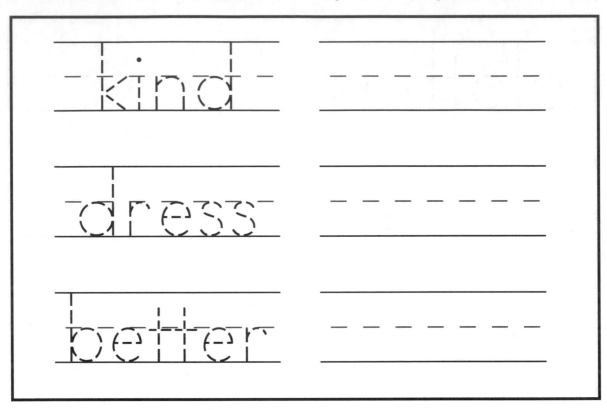

Directions: The words **kind**, **dress**, and **better** are hidden in the lines below. Find and circle them. Now, color the boxes.

k	n	d	k	i	n	d	n	k	i	n	d	n	i	k	n

r	s	e	d	s	r	d	r	e	s	s	d	r	e	s	s

b	e	b	e	t	t	e	r	b	t	b	e	t	t	e	r

Sight Word Vocabulary

Target words: clothes, coat, cold, kind, dress, better

Directions: Find and circle the words from the box. Words can go → or ↓.

| clothes |
| coat |
| cold |
| kind |
| dress |
| better |

r	c	k	i	n	d
b	l	r	c	o	r
e	o	h	o	o	e
t	t	a	a	c	s
t	h	m	t	h	s
e	e	p	e	s	r
r	s	c	o	l	d

Directions: Draw a line to connect each word to its picture.

1. kind

2. coat

3. clothes

4. dress

5. cold

6. better

Target words: **please, tell, once**

Directions: Write the words below. Say them as you write them.

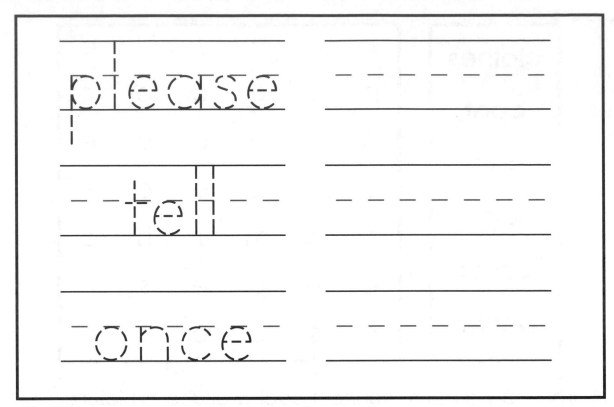

Directions: Write the missing word in each sentence. Use the words from the box to help you.

once	tell	please

1. Will you _____ close the door?

2. I can _____ time.

3. _____, I fell in a lake.

Target words: **use, made**

Directions: Write the words below. Say them as you write them.

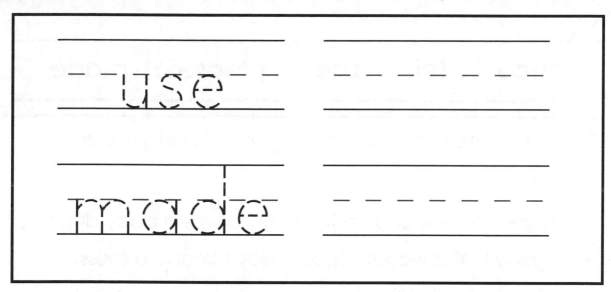

Directions: Write the missing word in each sentence. Use the words from the box to help you.

use	made

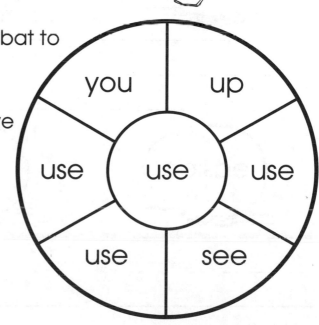

1. He _____ a home run hit.

2. I will _____ the bat to
   hit the ball.

Directions: Color the spaces that have
the same word as the one in the
middle of the circle.

you | up

use | use | use

use | see

Target words: please, tell, once, use, made

Directions: Read the story. Now, find and circle the words from the box.

once	tell	use	please	made

Once, I wanted to hear a story. I said, "Dad, please tell me one."

Dad said, "Once upon a time, there was a baby duck. It liked to play in the water. Once a day it made a mess. The mother duck said, "That is the last time I let you use the pond to swim in!"

Directions: Unscramble the words on the eggs.

 letl

 econ

 emda

_____

_____

_____

- -

_____

_____

_____

 easlpe

seu

_____

_____

- -

_____

_____

Target words: fly, fast, goes

Directions: Write the words below. Say them as you write them.

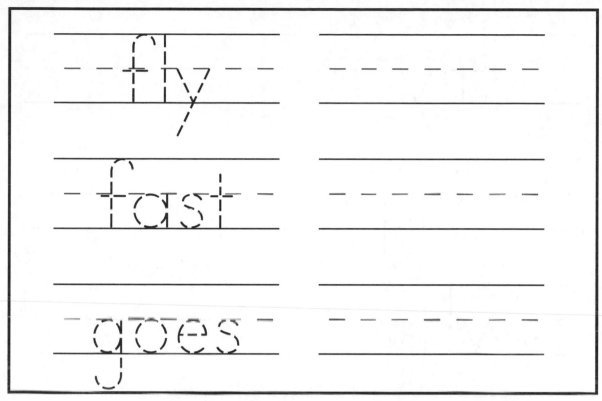

Directions: Color the spaces that have the same word as the one in the middle of the circle.

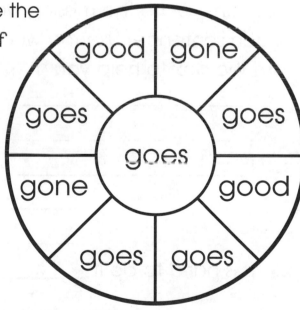

Now, write this sentence.

A plane can fly fast.

_____

— — — — — — — — — — —

_____

Target words: try, though, why

Directions: Write the words below. Say them as you write them.

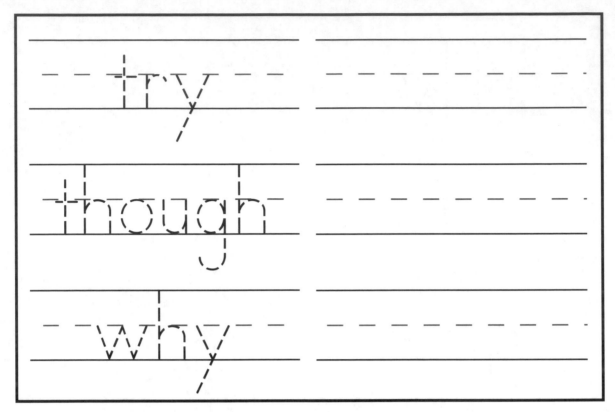

Directions: Write the missing word in each sentence. Use the words from the box to help you.

try	though	why

_____

‒ ‒ ‒ ‒ ‒ ‒ ‒ ‒

1. I _____ to tie my shoes.

_____

‒ ‒ ‒ ‒ ‒ ‒ ‒ ‒

2. It is hard to do it _____.

_____

‒ ‒ ‒ ‒ ‒ ‒ ‒ ‒

3. I don't know _____ it is hard to do.

Target words: fly, fast, goes, try, though, why

Directions: Find and circle the words from the box. Words can go → or ↓.

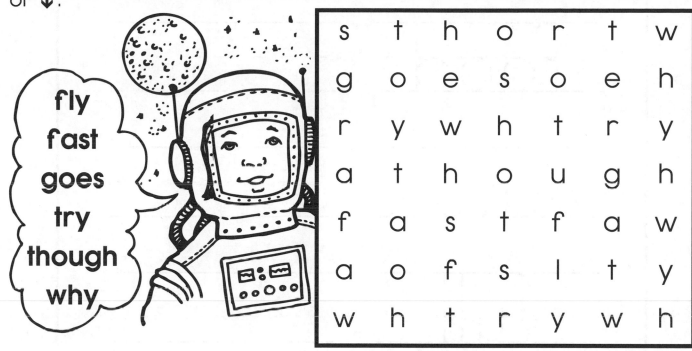

s	t	h	o	r	t	w
g	o	e	s	o	e	h
r	y	w	h	t	r	y
a	t	h	o	u	g	h
f	a	s	t	f	a	w
a	o	f	s	l	t	y
w	h	t	r	y	w	h

fly
fast
goes
try
though
why

Directions: Draw a line to connect the planes that have words that rhyme.

Target words: food, ate, full

Directions: Write the words below. Say them as you write them.

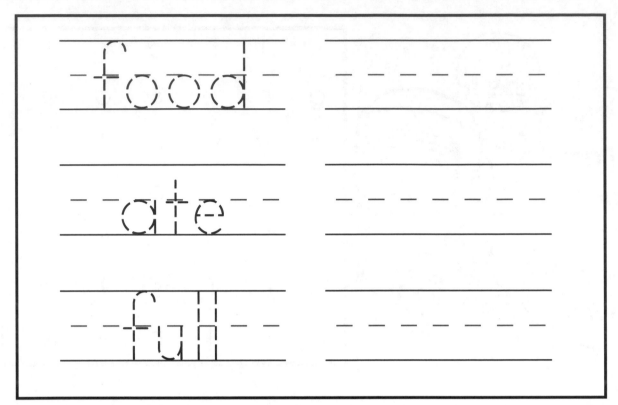

Directions: Write the missing word in each sentence.

food	ate	full

_____

1. I like to eat _____.

2. If I eat too much, I get _____.

3. Last night, I _____ too much.

Target words: most, more, always

Directions: Write the words below. Say them as you write them.

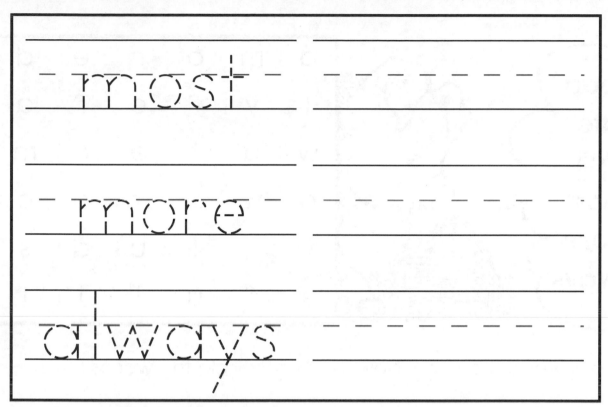

most

more

always

Directions: Write the missing letters from the words below. Use the words from the box to help you.

| most | more | always |

1. mo ____ t

2. a ____ way ____

3. mo ____ e

Now, write a sentence using one of the words from the box.

_____

- - - - - - - - - - - - - - - - - - - -

Target words: food, ate, full, most, more, always

Directions: Find and circle the words from the box. Words can go →
or ↓.

food
ate
full
most
more
always

a	m	o	r	e	d
l	y	f	e	f	a
w	a	t	e	o	m
a	w	t	m	o	o
y	l	l	u	d	s
s	f	u	l	l	t

Directions: Read the story. Now, find and circle the words from
the box.

This food is good. I always

eat too much. My dad eats the most.

One night he ate it all! Now he is

always full. He can not eat any more.

Sight Word Vocabulary

Target words: **write, letter, dear, love**

Directions: Write the words below. Say them as you write them.

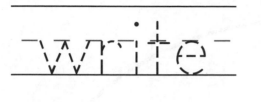

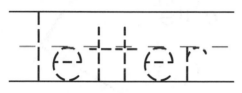

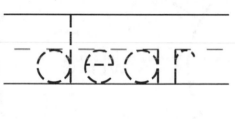

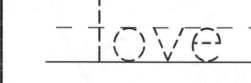

Directions: Answer the questions below using the words from the box.

letter   dear

1. What do you send in the mail? _____

2. What word do you use to begin a letter? _____

Target words: **write**

Directions: Color the spaces that have the same word as the one in the middle of the circle.

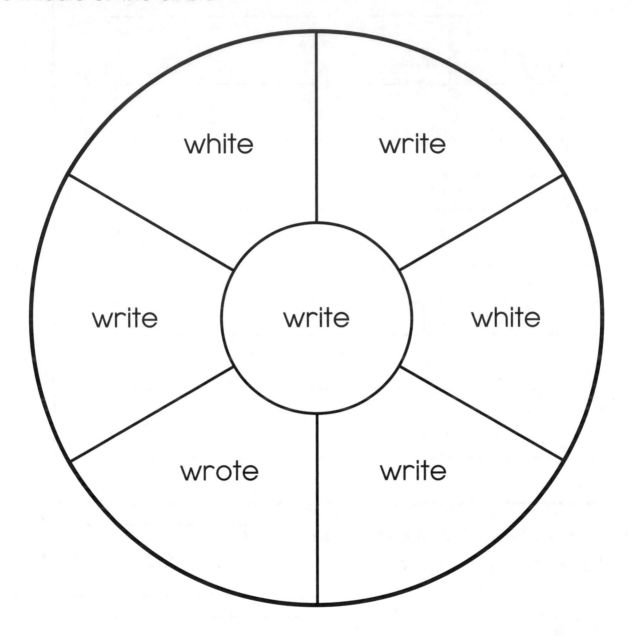

How many did you find? _____

Target words: yesterday, soon, fine

Directions: Write the words below. Say them as you write them.

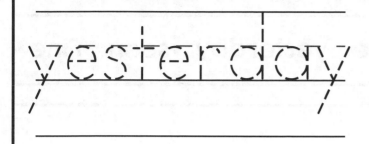

Directions: Circle the word that is the opposite of the underlined word.

1. I went home <u>yesterday</u>.   house   today   no

2. The bus will be here <u>soon</u>.   later   sun   hot

3. We are <u>fine</u>.   sing   song   sick

Now, write this sentence.
I was fine yesterday.

_____

- - - - - - - - - - - - - - - - - -

_____

Target words: write, letter, dear, love, yesterday, soon, fine

Directions: Find and circle the words from the box that are in the letter.

| write | letter | dear | love | yesterday | soon | fine |

Dear Grandmother,

   I want to write you a letter today because I miss you. I hope you are fine. Yesterday we went to the zoo. See you soon.

Love, Sam

Now, write a note to someone. Use the words **dear**, **love**, **soon**, and **fine**.

Target words: cut, grow, longer, keep

Directions: Write the words below. Say them as you write them.

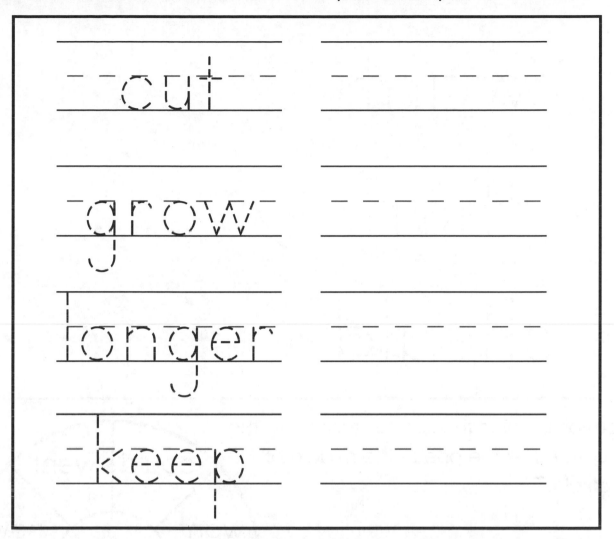

cut

grow

longer

keep

Directions: Find and circle the words from the box.

cut	grow	longer	keep

gone   grow   kite

kite   cat   longer

cat   keep

cut   gone

Target words: want, than, should

Directions: Write the words below. Say them as you write them.

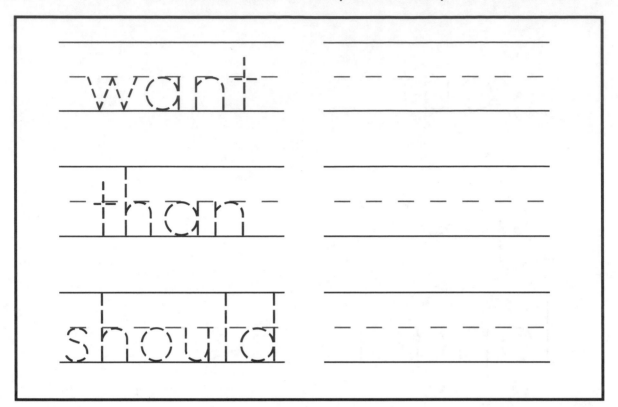

Directions: Color the spaces that have the same word as the one in the middle of the circle.

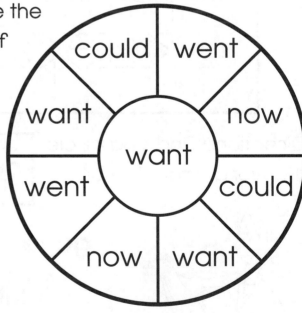

Now, write a sentence using the word **than** or **should**.

_____

- - - - - - - - - - - - -

Target words: cut, grow, longer, keep, want, than, should

Directions: Read the story. Find and circle the words from the box.

longer	keep	want	grow
should	cut	want	

I want to cut the grass. I should cut it today because it is going to rain. It is hard to keep it looking good. I want it to grow, but the bugs keep eating it. Maybe it will grow longer next year.

Directions: Write the letters that are missing in the words below. Use the words from the box to help you.

c ____ t   g ____ ow   t ____ a ____

____ ee ____   sh ____ ____ l ____   lo ____ ____ e ____

w ____ nt

Target words: these, thing, while

Directions: Write the words below. Say them as you write them.

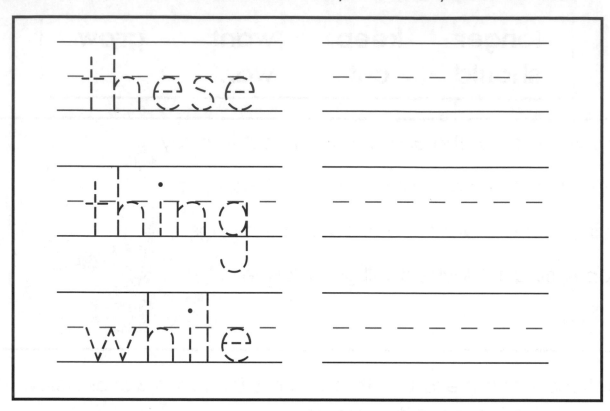

Directions: The words **these** and **thing** are hidden in the lines below. Find and circle them.

t	h	e	s	t	h	e	s	e	t	h	e	s	t	h	e

t	h	i	n	t	h	n	g	t	h	i	n	g	t	h	n

How many did you circle of each?

these _____   **thing** _____

Target words: **which, set**

Directions: Write the words below. Say them as you write them.

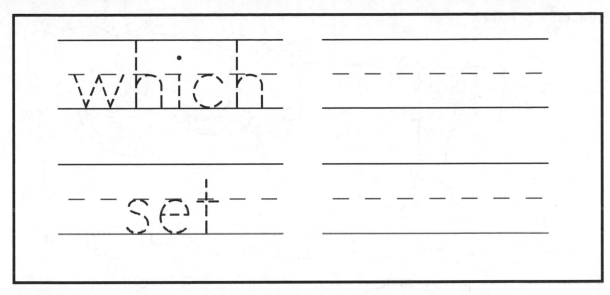

Directions: Color the spaces that have the same word as the one in the middle of the circle.

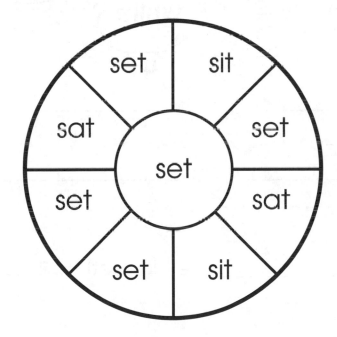

How many spaces did you color? _____

Target words: these, thing, while, which, set

Directions: Put the correct words on the footprints to complete the sentences below.

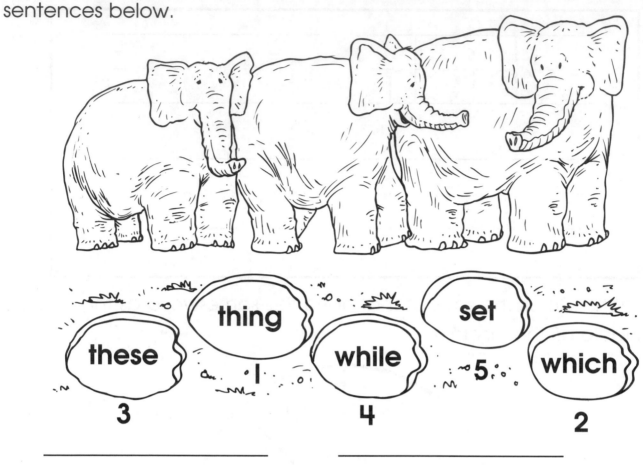

these 3

thing 1

while 4

set 5

which 2

_____
_ _ _ _ _ _ _

_____
_ _ _ _ _ _ _

This _____ is big. _____ animal is

_____
_ _ _ _ _ _ _

here? _____ are big feet! I will hide

_____
_ _ _ _ _ _ _

_____ it goes by. I do not want it to

_____
_ _ _ _ _ _ _

knock over my _____ of blocks.

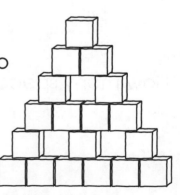

Sight Word Vocabulary

Target words: first, second, third

Directions: Write the words below. Say them as you write them.

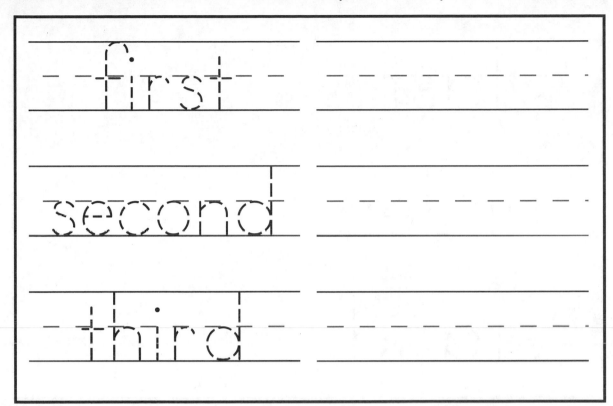

Directions: Write the word from the box that tells which football it is.

first	second	third

Directions: Answer the question below.

What grade are you in? _____

Target words: last, order, stand

Directions: Write the words below. Say them as you write them.

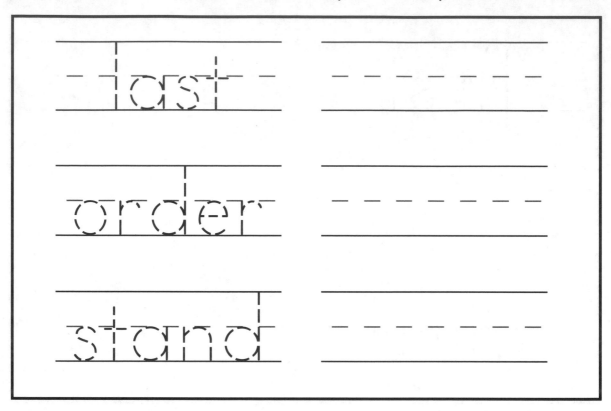

Directions: Answer the
questions using the words
from the box.

order	last	stand

1. Circle the dog that is next to last.

2. Color the dog that is on the stand.

3. The dogs are in order. Draw an arrow to show the tallest and the shortest dogs.

Target words: **first, second, third, last, order, stand**

Directions: Read the sentences to answer the questions about the picture.

1. Who is in the last row? _____

    _ _ _ _ _ _ _ _

2. Who is in the second row? _____

    _ _ _ _ _ _ _ _

3. Who is in the third row? _____

    _ _ _ _ _ _ _ _

4. Who is in the first row? _____

5. Draw where you will stand in the picture.

Target words: **where, does, those**

Directions: Write the words below. Say them as you write them.

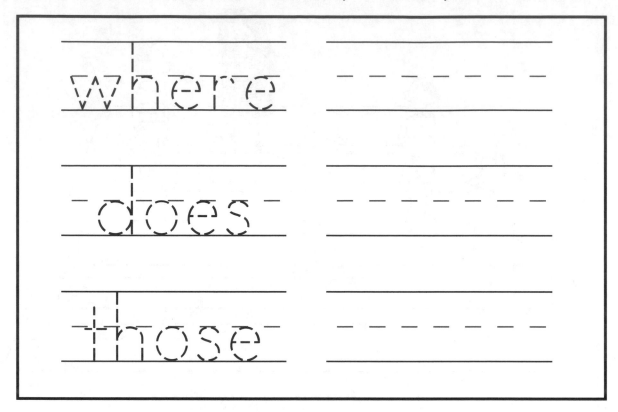

where _____

does _____

those _____

Directions: Write the word from the box that is missing in each sentence below.

| where | does | those |

_____

1. _____ he have his shoes?

_____

2. Are _____ his socks?

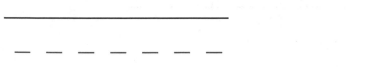

_____

3. _____ is his coat?

Target words: **now, seem, shall**

Directions: Write the words below. Say them as you write them.

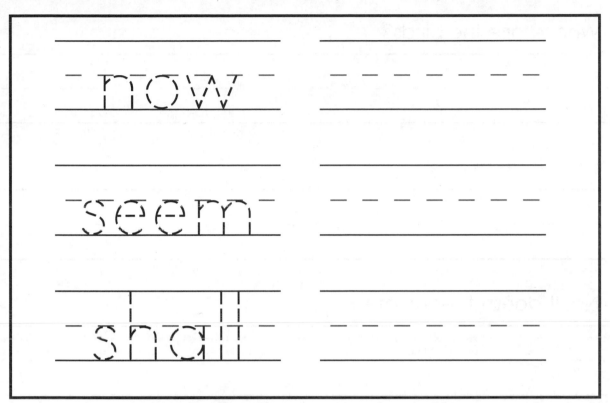

Directions: The words **now**, **seem**, and **shall** are hiding in the lines below. Find and circle them. Now, color the boxes.

n	w	o	n	o	w	o	w	n	o	w	n	o	n	o	w

e	m	e	e	m	s	e	e	m	e	e	s	e	e	m	e

s	h	l	l	s	h	a	l	l	s	h	a	l	s	h	a

Directions: What time is it now?

_____

_____

Target words: **where, does, those, now, seem, shall**

Directions: Write the sentences below.

1. Where are the birds?

2. Does it seem late?

3. No, it doesn't seem late.

4. What time is it now?

5. Who has those shoes?

6. Shall I open the door?

Target words: eyes, ear, hear

Directions: Write the words below. Say them as you write them.

```
_____          - - - - - - - - -
  eyes                    _____

_____          - - - - - - - - -
  ear                     _____

_____          - - - - - - - - -
  hear                    _____
```

Directions: Write the word that is missing in each sentence below.

| eyes | ear | hear |

1. I see with my _____.

2. My _____ can help me _____.

Now, draw a picture of your face. Show where your eyes and ears are. Put a label on them.

Target words: face, hand, head

Directions: Write the words below. Say them as you write them.

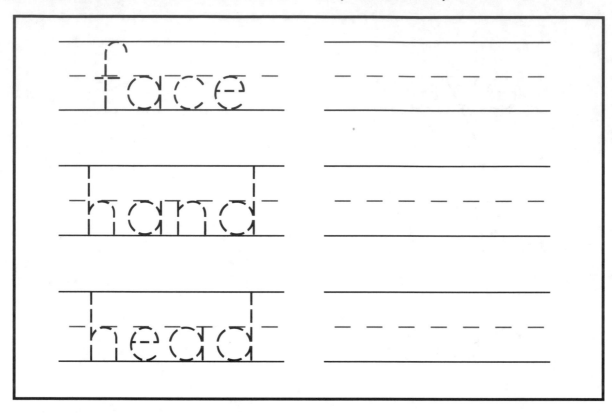

Directions: Fill in the letters that are missing in the words below.

1. h _____ n _____

2. f _____ c _____

3. h _____ _____ d

Now, draw a picture of yourself . Show where your face, hands, and head are. Put labels on your drawing.

Target words: eyes, ear, hear, face, hand, head

Directions: Use the words from the box to fill in the labels on the drawing.

eyes	ear	face
hand	head	

Now, write this sentence.

I can hear a train.

_____

_ _ _ _ _ _ _ _ _ _ _ _ _ _ _ _ _ _ _ _

Target words: **fire, sure, start**

Directions: Write the words below. Say them as you write them.

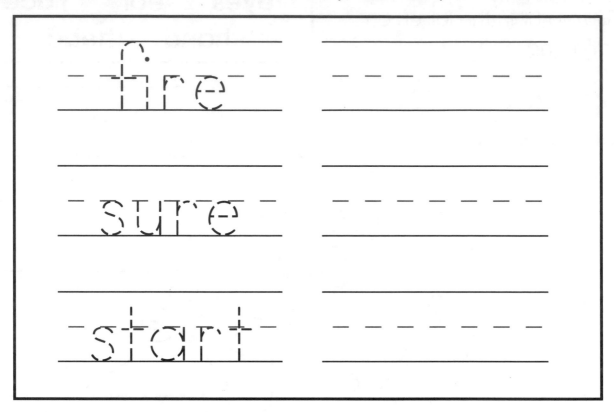

Directions: Color the spaces that have the same word as the one in the middle of the circle.

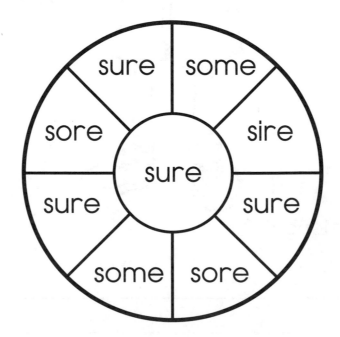

Target words: **hold, show, hope, start**

Directions: Write the words below. Say them as you write them.

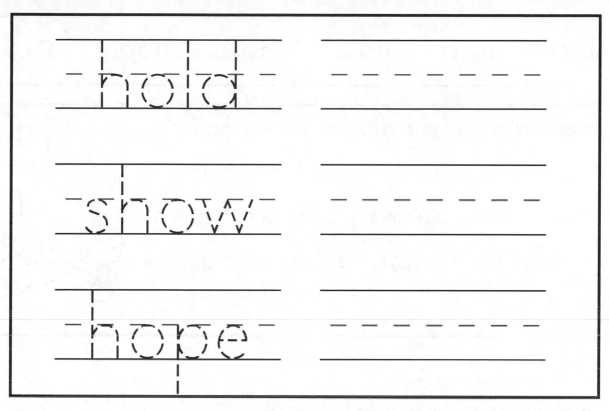

Directions: Circle the three words in each row that are the same.

hope	hold	hold	home	hold
shop	ship	show	show	show
home	hope	hope	ham	hope
start	stop	start	store	start

Target words: fire, sure, start, hold, show, hope

Directions: Read the story. Find and circle the words from the box.

start	sure	hold	show	hope	fire

It is cold and time to start a fire. My dad will show us how to start the fire. I hope it gets warm soon. I will hold my hands close to the fire to warm up. My dad says, "Be sure not to get too close."

Now, write this sentence.

I hope he will show us how to hold that.

_____

– – – – – – – – – – – – – – –

_____

– – – – – – – – – – – – – – –

_____

Target words: right, left, myself

Directions: Write the words below. Say them as you write them.

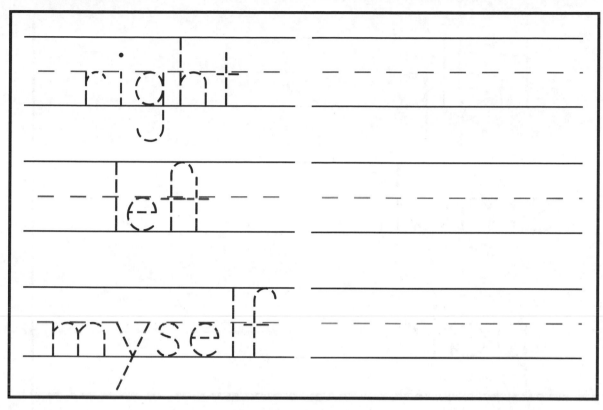

Directions: Read the sentences. Now, follow the directions.

1. Circle the dog on the right.

2. Color the dog on the left.

3. Draw an arrow to the cat on the left.

4. Color the cat on the right.

Now, complete this sentence.

I like myself because _____

_____

_____

Target words: help, small, pair

Directions: Write the words below. Say them as you write them.

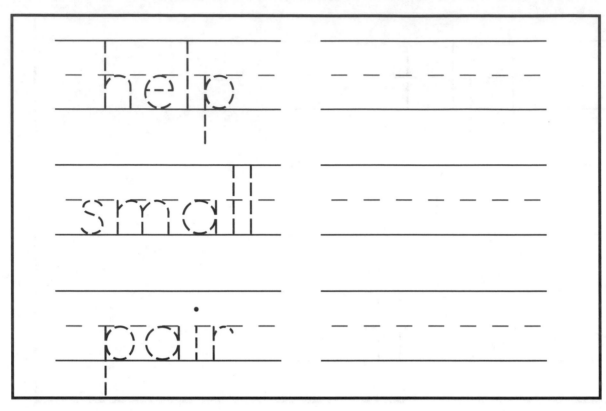

Directions: Draw a line to match the pants that have the same words on them.

help	small	pair

 help
 pair
 all
 small
 help
 hope
 small
 pair

Now, write this sentence.

It is a pair of pants.

_____

- -

_____

NAME _____

Target words: **right, left, myself, help, small, pair**

Directions: Find and circle the words from the box. Words can go →
or ↓.

right
left
myself
help
small
pair

m	y	s	e	l	f	f
t	t	l	p	f	r	t
s	m	a	l	l	r	f
g	f	p	e	e	i	e
h	e	l	p	f	g	l
l	s	m	a	t	h	g
p	a	i	r	m	t	h

Directions: Draw a line to connect words that are opposites.

yourself	hurt
right	pair
big	left
one	small
help	myself

Now, draw a picture of one of the opposite pairs.

Target words: came, gave, pretty

Directions: Write the words below. Say them as you write them.

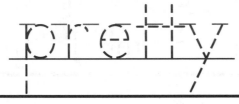
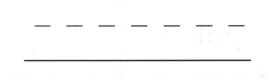

Directions: Write these sentences.

My friend came to my party.

Mother gave me a dress.

I had a pretty cake.

Sight Word Vocabulary

NAME _____

Target words: **present, bring, sing**

Directions: Write the words below. Say them as you write them.

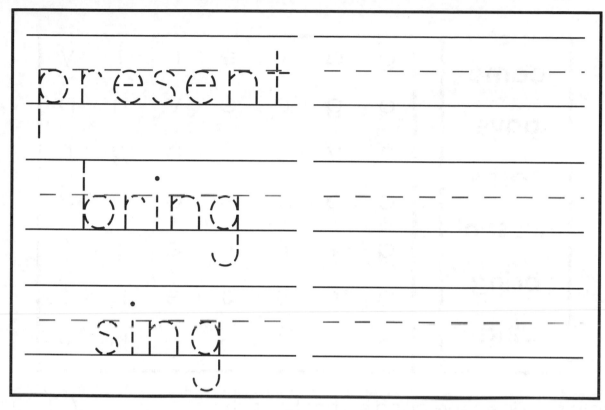

Directions: Color the boxes that have **present**, **bring**, and **sing** in them. Use a different color for each word.

song	present	bang	sing
pretty	bring	song	present
sing	present	bright	sang
present	pretty	sing	bring

How many did you find?

present _____   bring _____   sing _____

Spectrum Sight Words
Grade 1

Sight Word Vocabulary

97

Target words: came, gave, pretty, present, bring, sing

Directions: Find and circle the words from the box. Words can go →
or ↓.

came
gave
pretty
present
bring
sing

g	a	v	e	r	l	y
o	g	a	e	v	n	p
n	v	s	i	n	g	r
c	a	m	e	o	n	e
a	t	p	r	e	i	t
p	r	e	s	e	n	t
b	r	i	n	g	b	y

Directions: Circle the candles that have the
words from the box on them.

sing

came

song

come

pretty

present

gift

bring

give

gave

How many candles did you circle? _____

Target words: happy, wish, thank

Directions: Write the words below. Say them as you write them.

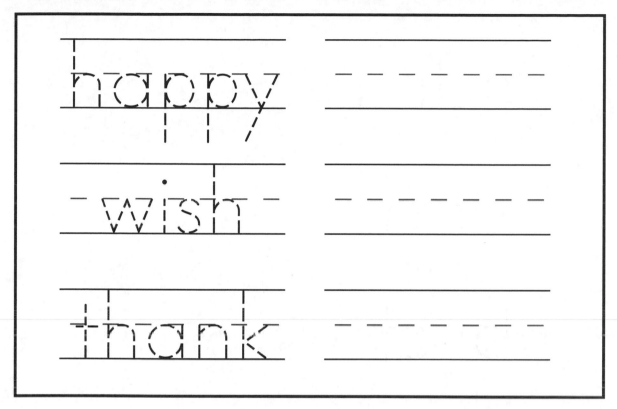

Directions: Draw a string to tie the balloons together that have the words from the box on them.

| happy | wish | thank |

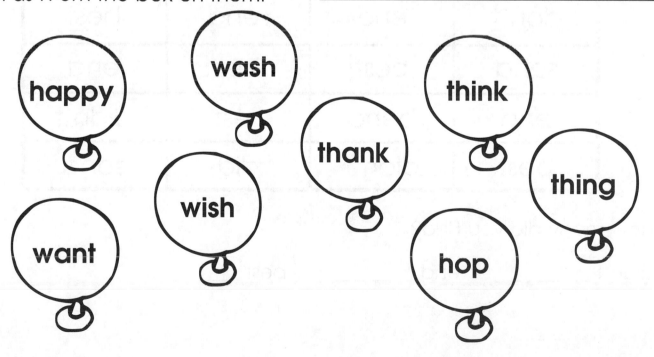

Target words: **didn't, end, best**

Directions: Write the words below. Say them as you write them.

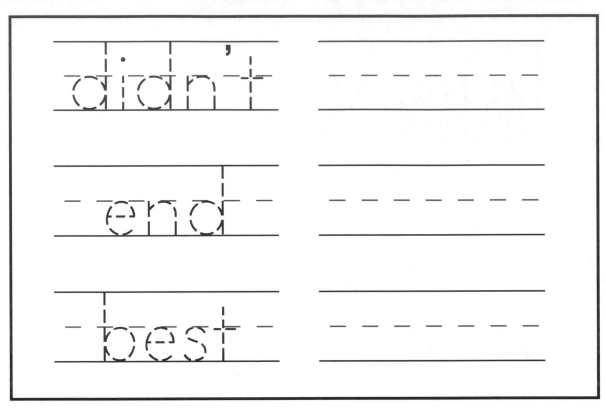

Directions: Color the boxes that have the words **didn't**, **end**, and **best** in them. Use a different color for each word.

don't	end	send	best
send	best	bet	end
end	bend	rest	didn't
best	didn't	did	send

How many did you find?

didn't _____   end _____   best _____

Target words: came, gave, pretty, present, bring, sing, happy, wish, thank, didn't, end, best

Directions: Read the story. Now, find and circle the words that are in the box.

came	gave	pretty	present	bring	sing
happy	wish	thank	didn't	end	best

It was my birthday. Lots of people came to bring me a present. They also came to sing happy birthday. My mother gave me a pretty dress. My brother gave me a big book. I have to thank them all. I wish the day didn't have to end. It was the best birthday ever!

Now, draw a picture of your favorite birthday present.

Cloze Sentences

Sight Word Cloze Sentences

Cloze sentences provide young learners an opportunity to use words in context and to gain a better understanding of sentence sense. Use the cloze sentences on the following pages for children to practice selecting the correct word from the word boxes to complete each sentence.

To extend the activity, have children create their own sentences with a missing word. The sentences can also be copied on a separate sheet of paper, cut apart, and reconstructed for sentence sense practice.

Directions: Write the missing word in each sentence.

big box got ran let

1. I _____ a dog.

2. He sleeps in a _____.

3. My dog is _____.

4. He _____ in the yard.

5. I _____ him lick me.

Cloze Sentences

Directions: Write the missing word in each sentence.

girl	look	find	sit	run	yes

1. The _____ had a dog.

2. The dog liked to _____ away fast.

3. The girl had to _____ the dog.

4. She had to _____ for him.

5. Did she find him? _____ , she did!

6. Now the girl wants the dog to _____ .

Cloze Sentences

Directions: Write the missing word in each sentence.

sleep	bed	morning	school	early	night

_____

1. It is dark at _____.

_____

2. I get in my _____.

_____

3. I have to go to _____ now.

_____

4. In the _____ I get up.

_____

5. I have to get up _____.

_____

6. And I have to go to _____.

Cloze Sentences

Directions: Write the missing word in each sentence.

open	close	leave	door	don't	off

1. I see a _____.

2. It is _____.

3. Don't _____ the door.

4. _____ the light on.

5. Please don't turn _____ the light.

6. I _____ like the dark.

Cloze Sentences

Directions: Write the missing word in each sentence.

car	far	ride	took	around	back

1. We went for a _____.

2. We drove in the _____.

3. The ride _____ a long time.

4. We went _____ away.

5. Then we went _____ the park.

6. At last we came _____ home.

Cloze Sentences

Directions: Write the missing word in each sentence.

done	wash	clean	water	carry	warm

1. I have to _____ the dishes.

2. I will _____ them to the sink.

3. I need to get some _____.

4. The water is not too _____.

5. Now the dishes are _____.

6. Now I am _____!

Cloze Sentences

Directions: Write the missing word in each sentence.

| coat | cold | dress | kind | better | clothes |

1. It is _____ outside.
   _ _ _ _ _ _ _ _ _ _

2. I _____ not go outside yet.
   _ _ _ _ _ _ _ _ _

3. My _____ is not very warm.
   _ _ _ _ _ _ _ _

4. First, I need to put on some warm _____.
   _ _ _ _ _ _ _ _

5. My mom gives me a warm _____.
   _ _ _ _ _ _ _ _

6. She is very _____ to me.
   _ _ _ _ _ _ _ _ _

Cloze Sentences

Directions: Write the missing word in each sentence.

more	always	ate	food	full	most

1. The _____ is good here.

2. I _____ eat too much.

3. My dad eats the _____ food.

4. He _____ all the food on his plate!

5. Now he is _____.

6. He can not eat any _____.

Cloze Sentences

Directions: Write the missing word in each sentence.

| dear | letter | soon | love | fine | yesterday |

1. Bob wrote a _____ to his sister.

2. He wrote, " _____ Pat, how are you?"

3. "I am _____," Bob wrote.

4. " _____ I went to the park."

5. He signed it, " _____, Bob."

6. He will mail it _____.

Cloze Sentences

Directions: Write the missing word in each sentence.

ear	hand	head	eyes	hear	face

_____
\- \- \- \- \- \- \- \- \- \-

1. I can _____ the dog bark.

_____
\- \- \- \- \- \- \- \- \-

2. I can hear with my _____.

_____
\- \- \- \- \- \- \- \- \-

3. I have two _____.

_____
\- \- \- \- \- \- \- \-

4. I can see my _____ in the mirror.

_____
\- \- \- \- \- \- \- \- \-

5. My hat is on my _____.

_____
\- \- \- \- \- \- \- \-

6. A _____ has five fingers.

NAME _____

Sight Word Scrambled Sentences

Once children can recognize and understand individual sight words in print, they are ready to use them to build sentences. This is the exciting next step in the reading process and, for many children, the moment when they say, "I'm really reading!"

The following scrambled sentences build upon sight word knowledge and are designed to help children learn—and demonstrate—sentence sense by putting individual words into the correct order so each sentence makes sense. The sight words used in these sentences follow the order in which they have been introduced.

The sentences can be used in a number of ways, depending on each child's developmental level. First, encourage the child to look for helpful sentence-sense clues, such as a capitalized word that would indicate the beginning of the sentence and a word with punctuation that would indicate the end of the sentence. Then, have the child say all the words aloud, starting with the capitalized word and ending with the punctuated word. Ask the child if what he or she said aloud makes sense, and, if necessary, encourage him or her to rearrange the "middle" words around while saying them aloud until they are in the correct order. Then, have the child write the unscrambled sentence on the line provided. You may want to encourage the child to write the sentence's sight words in different-colored crayons or markers, or to use the sight word flash cards to find the matching words used in the sentence.

You may also want to have the child write the unscrambled sentence on a separate sheet of paper and cut it apart into individual words. Then, using the child's hand-written unscrambled sentence in the workbook as a model, have him or her reassemble the cut-apart words into the sentence. This activity works well as a self-checking review. Or have the child distribute the cut-apart words to other children, who can then reassemble them in the correct order. An activity of this type can also be used with sentences that the children dictate or write themselves on a separate sheet of paper. Extending this activity to sentences that children compose themselves increases their level of engagement and provides an opportunity for individualizing their learning.

Scrambled Sentences

say   I   May   this?

_____

— — — — — — — — — — — — — — — — — — — —

_____

likes   He   fast.   run   to

_____

— — — — — — — — — — — — — — — — — — — —

_____

him.   had   to   She   for   look

_____

— — — — — — — — — — — — — — — — — — — —

_____

buy   she   Can   pencil?   a

_____

— — — — — — — — — — — — — — — — — — — —

_____

Scrambled Sentences

under   tree.   rock   a   A   is

_____

- - - - - - - - - - - - - - - - - -

_____

will   the   car.   I   leave

_____

- - - - - - - - - - - - - - - - - -

_____

door.   Please   the   close

_____

- - - - - - - - - - - - - - - - - -

_____

get   Let's   pumpkin.   another

_____

- - - - - - - - - - - - - - - - - -

_____

- - - - - - - - - - - - - - - - - -

_____

Scrambled Sentences

fast.   That   plane   can   fly

_____

- - - - - - - - - - - - - - - - - - - -

_____

dad   most.   the   eats   My

_____

- - - - - - - - - - - - - - - - - - - -

_____

five   hand   has   fingers.   A

_____

- - - - - - - - - - - - - - - - - - - -

_____

letter   will   write   a   I   you.   to

_____

- - - - - - - - - - - - - - - - - - - -

_____

_____

- - - - - - - - - - - - - - - - - - - -

Scrambled Sentences

a   He   run.   hit   home

_____

- -

_____

soon   write   letter.   I   will   a

_____

- -

_____

can   I   see   eyes.   with   my

_____

- -

_____

goes   here.   It   right

_____

- -

_____

Sight Word Flash Cards

On the following pages are flash cards for all of the sight words used in this book. For ease of use, they are presented in the order of introduction in the book. Laminating the cards would also help make them durable. Punching a hole in each card and keeping them on a ring for each child is also a good way to keep the cards organized and easy to use.

There are many ways to use these cards. Listed below are some games and activities to help children learn to recognize the sight words:

- Sort the cards by sight words with the same beginning letter

- Find sight words that rhyme, and write other words that rhyme with the sight words on a dry erase board or separate sheet of paper.

- Sort the cards to make pairs of sight words that begin with the same letter. Play the "Memory" game using these words—players don't get to keep the pair unless they can read both words. As an extension of this, also have players use the words in sentences.

- Use a timer to see how quickly each sight word is recognized. Begin with a small number of cards. Add more cards once increased speed and confidence is achieved.

- Put the sight words in alphabetical order.

- Come up with another word that begins with the same sound as each sight word.

am	big
box	ran
let	got
play	ball

hat	call
jump	sat
red	black
yellow	green

white	blue
brown	color
say	ask
friend	way

may	today
girl	look
find	dog
run	sit

yes	four
five	six
seven	eight
nine	ten

money	buy
next	near
under	upon
high	tree

found	until
into	same
hard	part
round	fat

funny	might
saw	only
such	never
live	house

home	mother
sister	brother
each	own
name	year

also	fall
sleep	morning
night	bed
o'clock	early

school	open
close	leave
off	door
don't	read

book	over
another	because
car	far
ride	around

back	away
town	took
every	anything
think	people

could	too
men	woman
along	stop
both	walk

clean	wash
water	carry
hot	warm
clothes	coat

cold	kind
dress	better
please	tell
once	use

made	fly
fast	goes
try	though
why	food

ate	full
most	more
always	write
letter	dear

love	yesterday
soon	fine
cut	grow
longer	keep

want	than
should	these
thing	while
which	set

first	second
third	last
order	stand
where	does

those	now
seem	shall
eyes	ear
hear	face

hand	head
fire	sure
start	hold
show	hope

right	left
myself	help
small	pair
come	gave

pretty	present
bring	sing
happy	wish
thank	didn't

end	best

Sight Word Flash Cards

Fry Instant Sight Word List

First One Hundred Words

a	can	her	many	see	us
about	come	here	me	she	very
after	day	him	much	so	was
again	did	his	my	some	we
all	do	how	new	take	were
an	down	I	no	that	what
and	eat	if	not	the	when
any	for	in	of	their	which
are	from	is	old	them	who
as	get	it	on	then	will
at	give	just	one	there	with
be	go	know	or	they	work
been	good	like	other	this	would
before	had	little	our	three	you
boy	has	long	out	to	your
but	have	make	put	two	
by	he	man	said	up	

Fry Instant Sight Word List

Second One Hundred Words

also	color	home	must	red	think
am	could	house	name	right	too
another	dear	into	near	run	tree
away	each	kind	never	saw	under
back	ear	last	next	say	until
ball	end	leave	night	school	upon
because	far	left	only	seem	use
best	find	let	open	shall	want
better	first	live	over	should	way
big	five	look	own	soon	where
black	found	made	people	stand	while
book	four	may	play	such	white
both	friend	men	please	sure	wish
box	girl	more	present	tell	why
bring	got	morning	pretty	than	year
call	hand	most	ran	these	
came	high	mother	read	thing	

Fry Instant Sight Word List

Third One Hundred Words

along	didn't	food	keep	sat	though
always	does	full	letter	second	today
anything	dog	funny	longer	set	took
around	don't	gave	love	seven	town
ask	door	goes	might	show	try
ate	dress	green	money	sing	turn
bed	early	grow	myself	sister	walk
brown	eight	hat	now	sit	warm
buy	every	happy	o'clock	six	wash
car	eyes	hard	off	sleep	water
carry	face	head	once	small	woman
clean	fall	hear	order	start	write
close	fast	help	pair	stop	yellow
clothes	fat	hold	part	ten	yes
coat	fine	hope	ride	thank	yesterday
cold	fire	hot	round	third	
cut	fly	jump	same	those	

Answer Key

5

Directions: Write the words below. Say them as you write them.

am	am
big	big
box	box

Directions: Write the missing word in each sentence.

1. I **am** good at playing with my dog.
2. My dog is **big**
3. He is in a **box**

Now, write a sentence with these words in it: **big   box**

Answers will vary.

6

Directions: Write the words below. Say them as you write them.

ran	ran
let	let
got	got

Directions: Write the missing word in each sentence.

1. I **got** a dog.
2. He **ran** in the yard.
3. I **let** him lick me.

Now, write a sentence with these words in it: **dog   got**

Answers will vary.

7

Directions: Find and circle the words from the box. Words can go → or ↓.

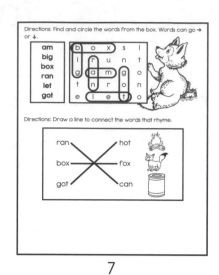

am
big
box
ran
let
got

Directions: Draw a line to connect the words that rhyme.

ran — hot
box — fox
got — can

8

Directions: Write the words below. Say them as you write them.

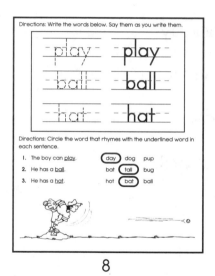

play	play
ball	ball
hat	hat

Directions: Circle the word that rhymes with the underlined word in each sentence.

1. The boy can <u>play</u>.   (day)   dog   pup
2. He has a <u>ball</u>.   bat   (tall)   bug
3. He has a <u>hat</u>.   hot   (bat)   ball

9

Directions: Write the words below. Say them as you write them.

call	call
jump	jump
sat	sat

Directions: Write the missing word in each sentence.

1. The frog can **jump**
2. He **sat** by the pond.
3. I will not **call** to him.
4. **Call** rhymes with **ball**.

10

Directions: Circle each set of footballs that have rhyming words on them.

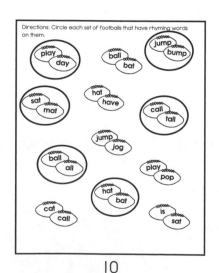

(play / day)   ball / bat   (jump / bump)
(sat / mat)   hat / have   (call / tall)
                jump / jog
(ball / all)   play / pop
(hat / bat)   cat / call   is / sat

11

Directions: Write the words below. Say them as you write them.

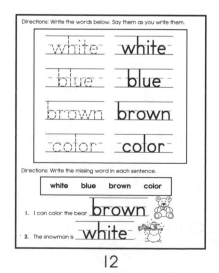

red	red
black	black
yellow	yellow
green	green

Directions: Write the missing word in each sentence.

1. A bear is **black**
2. An apple is **red/yellow/green**

12

Directions: Write the words below. Say them as you write them.

white	white
blue	blue
brown	brown
color	color

Directions: Write the missing word in each sentence.

| white | blue | brown | color |

1. I can color the bear **brown**
2. The snowman is **white**

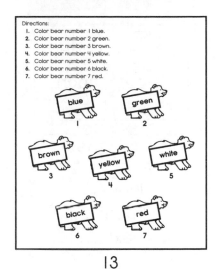

13

14

15

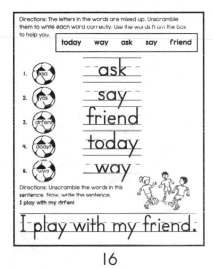

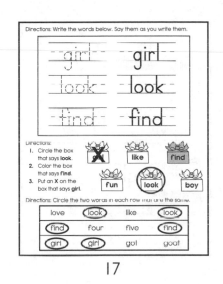

16

17

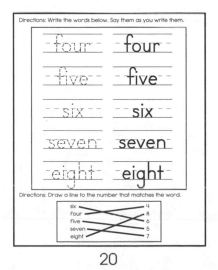

18

19

20

Answer Key

Directions: Write the words below. Say them as you write them.

nine	nine
ten	ten
money	money
buy	buy

Directions: Write the missing word in each sentence. Then, write the answers.

1. Can she __buy__ a pencil?

2. How much __money__ does she have?

21

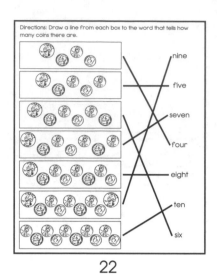

Directions: Draw a line from each box to the word that tells how many coins there are.

- nine
- five
- seven
- four
- eight
- ten
- six

22

Directions: Write the words below. Say them as you write them.

under	under
upon	upon
next	next
near	near

Directions: Write the missing word in each sentence.

1. The rock is __under/near__ a tree.

2. The frog sits __upon__ a lily pad.

3. The mouse is __next__ to the elephant.

23

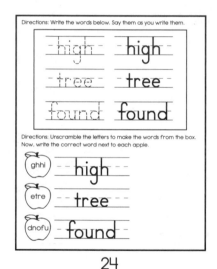

Directions: Write the words below. Say them as you write them.

high	high
tree	tree
found	found

Directions: Unscramble the letters to make the words from the box. Now, write the correct word next to each apple.

- ghhi — __high__
- etre — __tree__
- dnofu — __found__

24

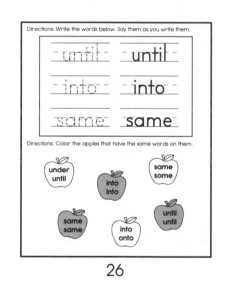

Directions: Write the words below. Say them as you write them.

until	until
into	into
same	same

Directions: Color the apples that have the same words on them.

- under until
- into into
- same some
- same same
- into onto
- until until

26

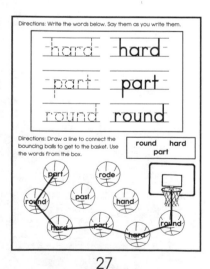

Directions: Write the words below. Say them as you write them.

hard	hard
part	part
round	round

Directions: Draw a line to connect the bouncing balls to get to the basket. Use the words from the box.

| round | hard |
| part | |

part, rode, round, past, hand, hard, part, round

27

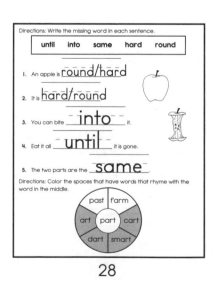

Directions: Write the missing word in each sentence.

| until | into | same | hard | round |

1. An apple is __round/hard__

2. It is __hard/round__

3. You can bite __into__ it.

4. Eat it all __until__ it is gone.

5. The two parts are the __same__

Directions: Color the spaces that have words that rhyme with the word in the middle.

- past farm
- art part cart
- dart smart

28

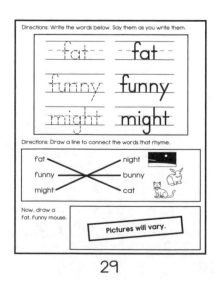

Directions: Write the words below. Say them as you write them.

fat	fat
funny	funny
might	might

Directions: Draw a line to connect the words that rhyme.

- fat — night
- funny — bunny
- might — cat

Now, draw a fat, funny mouse.

| Pictures will vary. |

29

Answer Key

Directions: Write the words below. Say them as you write them.

saw	saw
only	only
such	such
never	never

Directions: The words **saw**, **only**, **such**, and **never** are hiding in the boxes below. Find them and color the boxes that have these words in them.

one	only	on	only
saw	was	sun	saw
much	such	such	more
never	ever	never	even

30

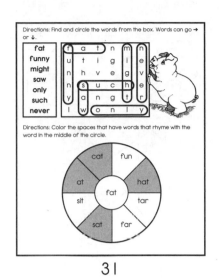

Directions: Find and circle the words from the box. Words can go → or ↓.

fat
funny
might
saw
only
such
never

Directions: Color the spaces that have words that rhyme with the word in the middle of the circle.

cat | fun
at | hat
fat
sit | tar
sat | far

31

Directions: Write the words below. Say them as you write them.

live	live
house	house
home	home

Directions: The letters on the houses are mixed up. Unscramble them to write each word. Use the words from the box to help you.

live   house
home

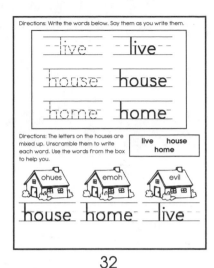

ohues   emoh   evil

house   home   live

32

Directions: Write the words below. Say them as you write them.

mother	mother
sister	sister
brother	brother

Directions: Select the word from the box that answers these riddles.

mother   sister   brother

I am a girl.   sister

I am a boy.   brother

I am a woman.   mother

Pictures will vary.

Now, draw a picture of yourself.

33

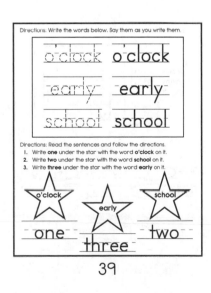

Directions: Find and circle the words from the box. Words can go → or ↓.

live
house
home
mother
sister

Directions: Draw a picture of where you live.

Pictures will vary.

34

each   own   name   year   also   fall

Directions: Find the leaves that have the words from the box on them. Color them these colors:

each = red   **own** = green   **name** = yellow
year = orange   **also** = brown

brown
red   green
orange
fall   yellow   red
orange
yellow   brown
green   fall

FALL

37

Directions: Write the words below. Say them as you write them.

o'clock	o'clock
early	early
school	school

Directions: Read the sentences and follow the directions.
1. Write **one** under the star with the word **o'clock** on it.
2. Write **two** under the star with the word **school** on it.
3. Write **three** under the star with the word **early** on it.

o'clock   early   school
one   three   two

39

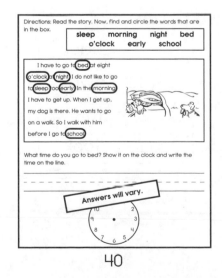

Directions: Read the story. Now, find and circle the words that are in the box.

sleep   morning   night   bed
o'clock   early   school

I have to go to bed at eight o'clock at night. I do not like to go to sleep too early. In the morning I have to get up. When I get up, my dog is there. He wants to go on a walk. So I walk with him before I go to school.

What time do you go to bed? Show it on the clock and write the time on the line.

Answers will vary.

40

Answer Key

Directions: Write the words below. Say them as you write them.

off off
door door
don't don't

Directions: Write the missing word in each sentence. Use the words from the box to help you.

| off | door | don't |

1. I will turn __off__ the light.
2. __Don't__ close the door.
3. The __door__ is open.

42

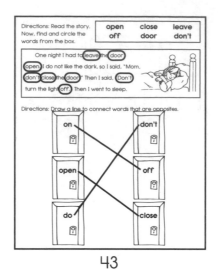

Directions: Read the story. Now, find and circle the words from the box.

| open | close | leave |
| off | door | don't |

One night I had to leave the (door) (open). I do not like the dark, so I said, "Mom, (don't) (close) the (door)." Then I said, (Don't) turn the light (off)." Then I went to sleep.

Directions: Draw a line to connect words that are opposites.

on — off
open — close
do — don't

43

Directions: Write the words below. Say them as you write them.

read
book
over

Directions: Several words below are mixed up. Unscramble the letters and write all the words on the lines. Use the words from the box.

| book | over | read | and | can | I | a |

I nac daer a kobo
I can read a book
voer dna voer.
over and over

44

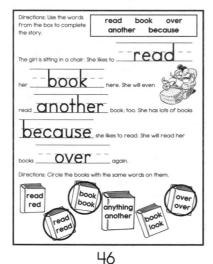

Directions: Use the words from the box to complete the story.

| read | book | over |
| another | because |

The girl is sitting in a chair. She likes to __read__ her __book__ here. She will even read __another__ book, too. She has lots of books __because__ she likes to read. She will read her books __over__ again.

Directions: Circle the books with the same words on them.

read red
book book
anything another
over over
read read
book look

46

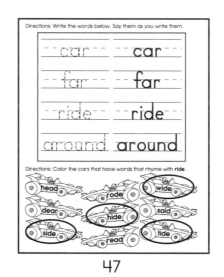

Directions: Write the words below. Say them as you write them.

car car
far far
ride ride
around around

Directions: Color the cars that have words that rhyme with **ride**.

head
rode
wide
dear
hide
said
side
read
tide

47

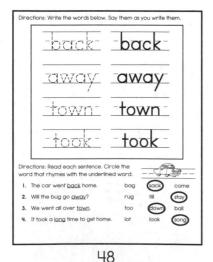

Directions: Write the words below. Say them as you write them.

back back
away away
town town
took took

Directions: Read each sentence. Circle the word that rhymes with the underlined word.

1. The car went <u>back</u> home. bag sack come
2. Will the bug go <u>away</u>? rug till stay
3. We went all over <u>town</u>. too down ball
4. It took a <u>long</u> time to get home. lot look song

48

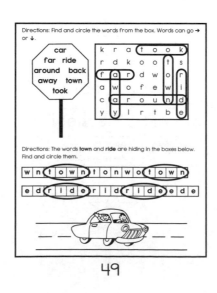

Directions: Find and circle the words from the box. Words can go → or ↓.

car
far ride
around back
away town
took

```
k r a t o o k
r d k o o t s
f a r d w o t
a w o f e w l
c a r o u n d
y y l r t b e
```

Directions: The words **town** and **ride** are hiding in the boxes below. Find and circle them.

w n t o w n t o n w o t o w n
e d r i d e r i d r i d e e d e

49

Directions: Write the words below. Say them as you write them.

every every
anything anything
think think

Directions: Color the spaces that have the same word as the one in the middle of the circle.

even every
ever every
every even
ever every

How many spaces did you color? __4__

50

Answer Key

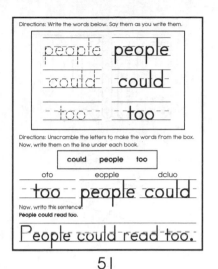

Directions: Write the words below. Say them as you write them.

people — people
could — could
too — too

Directions: Unscramble the letters to make the words from the box. Now, write them on the line under each book.

could   people   too

oto — too
eopple — people
dcluo — could

Now, write this sentence:
People could read too.

People could read too.

51

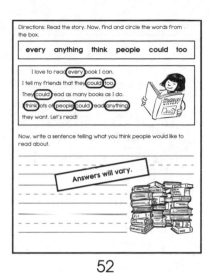

Directions: Read the story. Now, find and circle the words from the box.

every   anything   think   people   could   too

I love to read every book I can.
I tell my friends that they could too.
They could read as many books as I do.
think lots of people could read anything
they want. Let's read!

Now, write a sentence telling what you think people would like to read about.

Answers will vary.

52

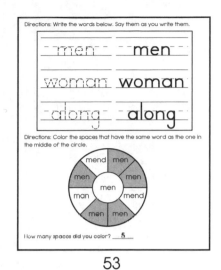

Directions: Write the words below. Say them as you write them.

men — men
woman — woman
along — along

Directions: Color the spaces that have the same word as the one in the middle of the circle.

mend | men
men | men
man | mend
men | men

(center: men)

How many spaces did you color?   5

53

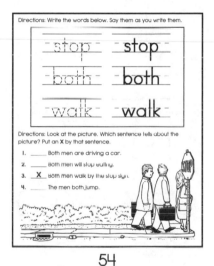

Directions: Write the words below. Say them as you write them.

stop — stop
both — both
walk — walk

Directions: Look at the picture. Which sentence tells about the picture? Put an X by that sentence.

1. _____ Both men are driving a car.
2. _____ Both men will stop eating.
3. _X_ Both men walk by the stop sign.
4. _____ The men both jump.

54

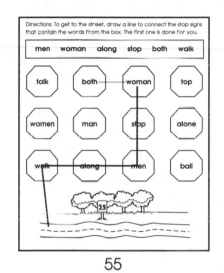

Directions: To get to the street, draw a line to connect the stop signs that contain the words from the box. The first one is done for you.

men   woman   along   stop   both   walk

talk   both   woman   top
women   man   stop   alone
walk   along   men   ball

(25)

55

Directions: Write the words below. Say them as you write them.

clean — clean
wash — wash
water — water

Directions: Unscramble the words on the wash tubs. Now, write each word on the line. Use the words from the box to help you.

swha   retwa   enacl

wash   water   clean

Now, write this sentence:
Wash with clean water.

Wash with clean water.

56

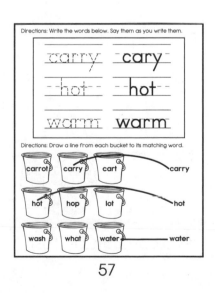

Directions: Write the words below. Say them as you write them.

cary — cary
hot — hot
warm — warm

Directions: Draw a line from each bucket to its matching word.

carrot   carry   cart ————— carry
hot   hop   lot ————— hot
wash   what   water ————— water

57

Directions: Unscramble the words from the box. Write each word on the line under its bubble. Now, write the words on the wash tubs in alphabetical order.

clean   wash   water   hot   warm

clean   naelc   hwas
hot
warm   rweat   toh
wash   clean   wash
water   awrm

water   hot

warm

58

59

Directions: Write the words below. Say them as you write them.

clothes — clothes
coat — coat
cold — cold

Directions: Color the spaces that have words that rhyme with the same word in the middle of the circle.

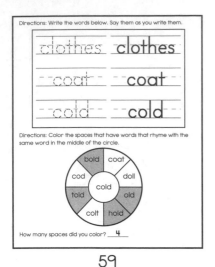

bold	coat
cod	doll
told	old
colt	hold

(center: cold)

How many spaces did you color? __4__

60

Directions: Write the words below. Say them as you write them.

kind — kind
dress — dress
better — better

Directions: The words **kind**, **dress**, and **better** are hidden in the lines below. Find and circle them. Now, color the boxes.

k n d (k i n d) n (k i n d) n i k n
r s e d s r (d r e s s) (d r e s s)
b e (b e t t e r) b t (b e t t e r)

61

Directions: Find and circle the words from the box. Words can go → or ↓.

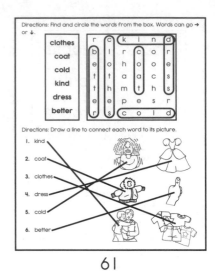

| clothes |
| coat |
| cold |
| kind |
| dress |
| better |

Directions: Draw a line to connect each word to its picture.

1. kind
2. coat
3. clothes
4. dress
5. cold
6. better

62

Directions: Write the words below. Say them as you write them.

please — please
tell — tell
once — once

Directions: Write the missing word in each sentence. Use the words from the box to help you.

once   tell   please

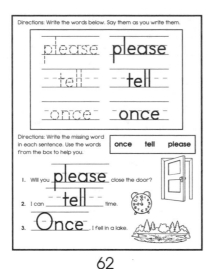

1. Will you **please** close the door?
2. I can **tell** time.
3. **Once** I fell in a lake.

63

Directions: Write the words below. Say them as you write them.

use — use
made — made

Directions: Write the missing word in each sentence. Use the words from the box to help you.

use   made

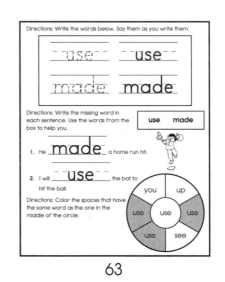

1. He **made** a home run hit.
2. I will **use** the bat to hit the ball.

Directions: Color the spaces that have the same word as the one in the middle of the circle.

you	up
use	use	use
use	see

(center: use)

64

Directions: Read the story. Now, find and circle the words from the box.

once   tell   use   please   made

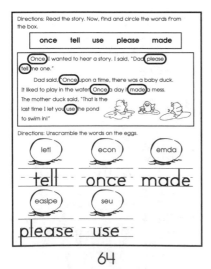

(Once) I wanted to hear a story. I said, "Dad, (please) (tell) me one."

Dad said, "(Once) upon a time, there was a baby duck. It liked to play in the water. (Once) a day it (made) a mess. The mother duck said, "That is the last time I let you (use) the pond to swim in!"

Directions: Unscramble the words on the eggs.

let! — **tell**
econ — **once**
emda — **made**
easlpe — **please**
seu — **use**

65

Directions: Write the words below. Say them as you write them.

fly — fly
fast — fast
goes — goes

Directions: Color the spaces that have the same word as the one in the middle of the circle.

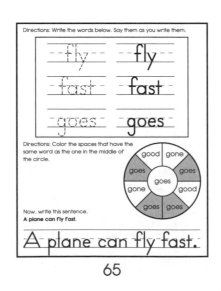

good	gone
goes	goes
goes	good
goes	goes

(center: goes)

Now, write this sentence.
A plane can fly fast.

A plane can fly fast.

66

Directions: Write the words below. Say them as you write them.

try — try
though — though
why — why

Directions: Write the missing word in each sentence. Use the words from the box to help you.

try   though   why

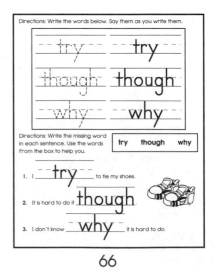

1. I **try** to tie my shoes.
2. It is hard to do it **though**.
3. I don't know **why** it is hard to do.

Answer Key

Directions: Find and circle the words from the box. Words can go → or ↓.

fly
fast
goes
try
though
why

s	t	h	o	r	t	w
g	o	e	s	o	e	h
r	y	w	h	t	r	y
a	t	h	o	u	g	h
f	a	s	t	s	l	t
a	o	f	s	l	t	y
w	h	t	r	y	w	h

Directions: Draw a line to connect the planes that have words that rhyme.

though · why
fly
try
goes · fast

67

Directions: Write the words below. Say them as you write them.

food food
ate ate
full full

Directions: Write the missing word in each sentence.

food   ate   full

1. I like to eat **food**.
2. If I eat too much, I get **full**.
3. Last night, I **ate** too much.

68

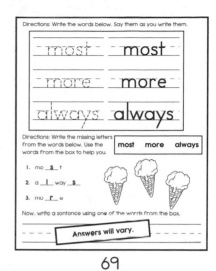

Directions: Write the words below. Say them as you write them.

most most
more more
always always

Directions: Write the missing letters from the words below. Use the words from the box to help you.

most   more   always

1. mo **s** t
2. a **l** way **s**
3. mo **r** e

Now, write a sentence using one of the words from the box.

_____ Answers will vary.

69

Directions: Find and circle the words from the box. Words can go → or ↓.

food
ate
full
most
more
always

a	m	o	r	e	d
l	y	f	e	f	a
w	a	t	e	o	m
a	w	t	m	o	o
y	s	l	l	u	s
s	f	u	l	l	t

Directions: Read the story. Now, find and circle the words from the box.

This **food** is good. I **always** eat too much. My dad eats the **most**. One night he **ate** it all! Now he is **always full**! He can not eat any **more**.

70

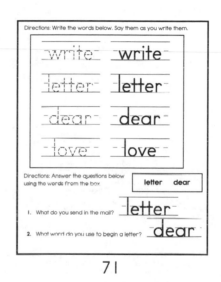

Directions: Write the words below. Say them as you write them.

write write
letter letter
dear dear
love love

Directions: Answer the questions below using the words from the box.

letter   dear

1. What do you send in the mail? **letter**
2. What word do you use to begin a letter? **dear**

71

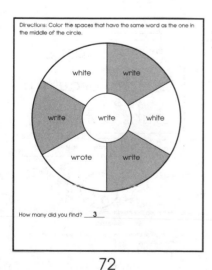

Directions: Color the spaces that have the same word as the one in the middle of the circle.

white | write
write | white
wrote | write
(center: write)

How many did you find? **3**

72

Directions: Write the words below. Say them as you write them.

yesterday yesterday
soon soon
fine fine

Directions: Circle the word that is the opposite of the underlined word.

1. I went home _yesterday_.   house   (today)   no
2. The bus will be here _soon_.   (later)   sun   hot
3. We are _fine_.   sing   song   (sick)

Now, write this sentence.
I was fine yesterday.

I was fine yesterday.

73

Directions: Find and circle the words from the box that are in the letter.

write   letter   dear   love   yesterday   soon   fine

(Dear) Grandmother,
I want to (write) you a (letter) today because I miss you. I hope you are (fine). (Yesterday) we went to the zoo. See you (soon).
(Love,) Sam

Now, write a note to someone. Use the words **dear, love, soon,** and **fine**.

Answers will vary.

74

Directions: Write the words below. Say them as you write them.

cut	cut
grow	grow
longer	longer
keep	keep

Directions: Find and circle the words from the box.

cut grow longer keep

gone   (grow)   kite
kite   cat   (longer)
cat   (keep)
(cut)   gone

75

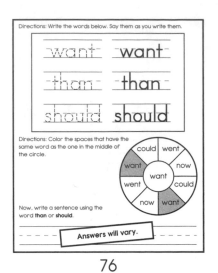

Directions: Write the words below. Say them as you write them.

want	want
than	than
should	should

Directions: Color the spaces that have the same word as the one in the middle of the circle.

could | went
want | now
want
went | could
now | want

Now, write a sentence using the word **than** or **should**.

_____ | Answers will vary.

76

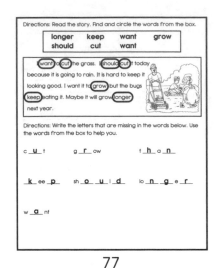

Directions: Read the story. Find and circle the words from the box.

| longer | keep | want | grow |
| should | cut | want | |

(want) to (cut) the grass. (should) (cut) it today because it is going to rain. It is hard to keep it looking good. I want it to (grow) but the bugs (keep) eating it. Maybe it will grow (longer) next year.

Directions: Write the letters that are missing in the words below. Use the words from the box to help you.

c _u_ t   g _r_ ow   t _h a_ n

k _ee_ p   sh _o u l_ d   lo _n g_ e r

w _a_ nt

77

Directions: Write the words below. Say them as you write them.

these	these
thing	thing
while	while

Directions: The words **these** and **thing** are hidden in the lines below. Find and circle them.

| t | h | e | s | t | (t | h | e | s | e) | t | h | e | s | t | h | e |
| t | h | i | n | t | h | n | g | (t | h | i | n | g) | t | h | n |

How many did you circle of each?

these __1__   thing __1__

78

Directions: Write the words below. Say them as you write them.

| which | which |
| set | set |

Directions: Color the spaces that have the same word as the one in the middle of the circle.

set | sit
sat | set
set
set | sat
set | sit

How many spaces did you color? __4__

79

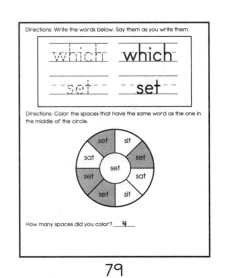

Directions: Put the correct words on the footprints to complete the sentences below.

these   thing   while   set   which
  3   4   2

This _thing_ is big. _Which_ animal is here? _These_ are big feet! I will hide _while_ it goes by. I do not want it to knock over my _set_ of blocks.

80

Directions: Write the words below. Say them as you write them.

first	first
second	second
third	third

Directions: Write the word from the box that tells which football it is.

first   second   third

first   _second_   _third_

Directions: Answer the question below.

What grade are you | Answers will vary.

81

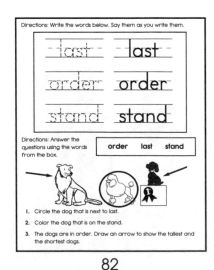

Directions: Write the words below. Say them as you write them.

last	last
order	order
stand	stand

Directions: Answer the questions using the words from the box.

order   last   stand

1. Circle the dog that is next to last.
2. Color the dog that is on the stand.
3. The dogs are in order. Draw an arrow to show the tallest and the shortest dogs.

82

Answer Key

83

Directions: Read the sentences to answer the questions about the picture.

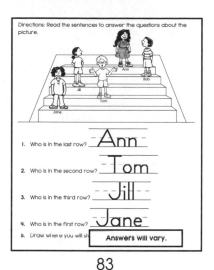

1. Who is in the last row? **Ann**
2. Who is in the second row? **Tom**
3. Who is in the third row? **Jill**
4. Who is in the first row? **Jane**
5. Draw where you will sl... **Answers will vary.**

84

Directions: Write the words below. Say them as you write them.

where	where
does	does
those	those

Directions: Write the word from the box that is missing in each sentence below.

where   does   those

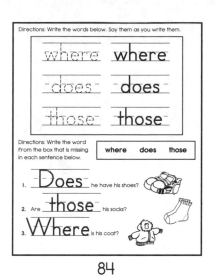

1. **Does** he have his shoes?
2. Are **those** his socks?
3. **Where** is his coat?

85

Directions: Write the words below. Say them as you write them.

now	now
seem	seem
shall	shall

Directions: The words **now**, **seem**, and **shall** are hiding in the lines below. Find and circle them. Now, color the boxes.

n w o (n o w) o w (n o w) n o (n o w)
e m e e m (s e e m) e e s (s e e m) e
s h l l (s h a l l) s h a l s h a

Directions: What time is it now?

nine o'clock / 9:00

87

Directions: Write the words below. Say them as you write them.

eyes	eyes
ear	ear
hear	hear

Directions: Write the word that is missing in each sentence below.

eyes   ear   hear

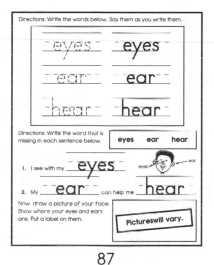

1. I see with my **eyes**
2. My **ear** can help me **hear**

Now, draw a picture of your face. Show where your eyes and ears are. Put a label on them.

Pictures will vary.

88

Directions: Write the words below. Say them as you write them.

face	face
hand	hand
head	head

Directions: Fill in the letters that are missing in the words below.

1. h **a** n **d**
2. f **a** c **e**
3. h **e** **a** d

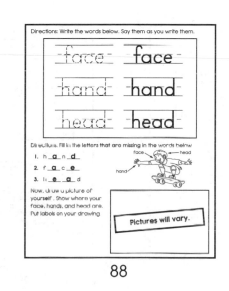

Now, draw a picture of yourself. Show where your face, hands, and head are. Put labels on your drawing.

Pictures will vary.

89

Directions: Use the words from the box to fill in the labels on the drawing.

**eyes   ear   face
hand   head**

head
eyes
ear
face
hand

Now, write this sentence.
I can hear a train.

I can hear a train.

90

Directions: Write the words below. Say them as you write them.

fire	fire
sure	sure
start	start

Directions: Color the spaces that have the same word as the one in the middle of the circle.

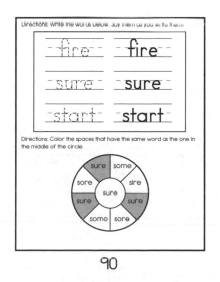

sure | some
sore | sire
sure | sure
some | sore

(center: sure)

91

Directions: Write the words below. Say them as you write them.

hold	hold
show	show
hope	hope

Directions: Circle the three words in each row that are the same.

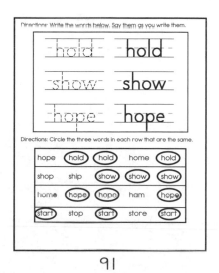

hope	(hold)	(hold)	home	(hold)
shop	ship	(show)	(show)	(show)
home	(hope)	(hope)	ham	(hope)
(start)	stop	(start)	store	(start)

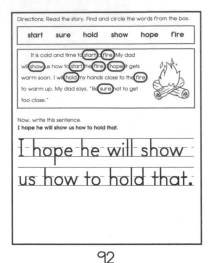

Directions: Read the story. Find and circle the words from the box.

start	sure	hold	show	hope	fire

It is cold and time to start a fire. My dad will show us how to start the fire. I hope it gets warm soon. I will hold my hands close to the fire to warm up. My dad says, "Be sure not to get too close."

Now, write this sentence.
I hope he will show us how to hold that.

I hope he will show us how to hold that.

92

Directions: Write the words below. Say them as you write them.

right	right
left	left
myself	myself

Directions: Read the sentences. Now, follow the directions.

1. Circle the dog on the right.
2. Color the dog on the left.
3. Draw an arrow to the cat on the left.
4. Color the cat on the right.

Now, complete this sentence.

I like myself because _____
Answers will vary.

93

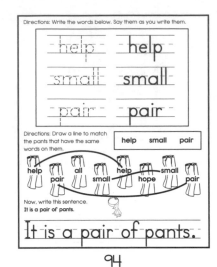

Directions: Write the words below. Say them as you write them.

help	help
small	small
pair	pair

Directions: Draw a line to match the pants that have the same words on them.

help	small	pair

help   pair   all   small   hope   small   pair

Now, write this sentence.
It is a pair of pants.

It is a pair of pants.

94

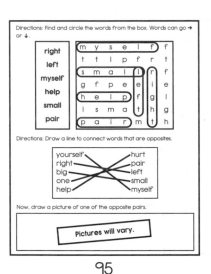

Directions: Find and circle the words from the box. Words can go → or ↓.

right	m y s e l f f
left	t t l p f r t
myself	s m a l l r n
help	g f p e e i e
small	h e l p f g l
pair	l s m a t h h
	p a i r m t h

Directions: Draw a line to connect words that are opposites.

yourself — hurt
right — pair
big — left
one — small
help — myself

Now, draw a picture of one of the opposite pairs.

Pictures will vary.

95

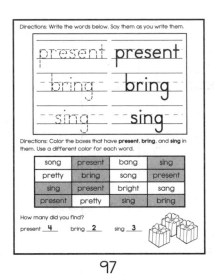

Directions: Write the words below. Say them as you write them.

present	present
bring	bring
sing	sing

Directions: Color the boxes that have **present**, **bring**, and **sing** in them. Use a different color for each word.

song	present	bang	sing
pretty	bring	song	present
sing	present	bright	sang
present	pretty	sing	bring

How many did you find?
present **4**   bring **2**   sing **3**

97

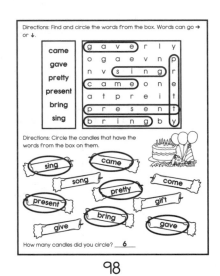

Directions: Find and circle the words from the box. Words can go → or ↓.

came	g a v e r l y
gave	o g a e v n p
pretty	n v s i n g r
present	c a m e o n e
bring	a t p r e i t
sing	p r e s e n t
	b r i n g b y

Directions: Circle the candles that have the words from the box on them.

sing   came   song   pretty   come   present   gift   bring   give   gave

How many candles did you circle? **6**

98

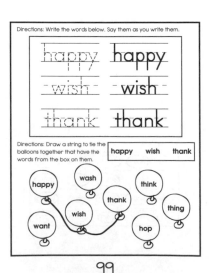

Directions: Write the words below. Say them as you write them.

happy	happy
wish	wish
thank	thank

Directions: Draw a string to tie the balloons together that have the words from the box on them.

happy	wish	thank

happy   wash   think   thank   thing   wish   hop   want

99

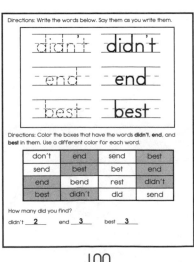

Directions: Write the words below. Say them as you write them.

didn't	didn't
end	end
best	best

Directions: Color the boxes that have the words **didn't**, **end**, and **best** in them. Use a different color for each word.

don't	end	send	best
send	best	bet	end
end	bend	rest	didn't
best	didn't	did	send

How many did you find?
didn't **2**   end **3**   best **3**

100

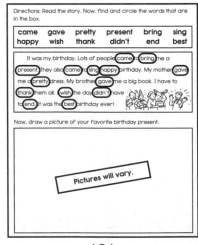

Directions: Read the story. Now, find and circle the words that are in the box.

came	gave	pretty	present	bring	sing
happy	wish	thank	didn't	end	best

It was my birthday. Lots of people came to bring me a present. They also came to sing happy birthday. My mother gave me a pretty dress. My brother gave me a big book. I have to thank them all. I wish the day didn't have to end. It was the best birthday ever!

Now, draw a picture of your favorite birthday present.

Pictures will vary.

101

Answer Key

Page 102
1. I <u>got</u> a dog.
2. He sleeps in a <u>box</u>.
3. My dog is <u>big</u>.
4. He <u>ran</u> in the yard.
5. I <u>let</u> him lick me.

Page 103
1. The <u>girl</u> had a dog.
2. The dog liked to <u>run</u> away fast.
3. The girl had to <u>find</u> the dog.
4. She had to <u>look</u> for him.
5. Did she find him? <u>Yes</u>, she did!
6. Now the girl wants the dog to <u>sit</u>.

Page 104
1. It is dark at <u>night</u>.
2. I get in my <u>bed</u>.
3. I have to go to <u>sleep</u> now.
4. In the <u>morning</u> I get up.
5. I have to get up <u>early</u>.
6. And I have to go to <u>school</u>.

Page 105
1. I see a <u>door</u>.
2. It is <u>open</u>.
3. Don't <u>close</u> the door.
4. <u>Leave</u> the light on.
5. Please don't turn <u>off</u> the light.
6. I <u>don't</u> like the dark.

Page 106
1. We went for a <u>ride</u>.
2. We drove in the <u>car</u>.
3. The ride <u>took</u> a long time.
4. We went <u>far</u> away.
5. Then we went <u>around</u> the park.
6. At last we came <u>back</u> home.

Page 107
1. I have to <u>wash</u> the dishes.
2. I will <u>carry</u> them to the sink.
3. I need to get some <u>water</u>.
4. The water is not too <u>warm</u>.
5. Now the dishes are <u>clean</u>.
6. Now I am <u>done</u>!

Page 108
1. It is <u>cold</u> outside.
2. I <u>better</u> not go outside yet.
3. My <u>dress</u> is not very warm.
4. First, I need to put on some warm <u>clothes</u>.
5. My mom gives me a warm <u>coat</u>.
6. She is very <u>kind</u> to me.

Page 109
1. The <u>food</u> is good here.
2. I <u>always</u> eat too much.
3. My dad eats the <u>most</u> food.
4. He <u>ate</u> all the food on his plate!
5. Now he is <u>full</u>.
6. He can not eat any <u>more</u>.

Page 110
1. Bob wrote a <u>letter</u> to his sister.
2. He wrote, "<u>Dear</u> Pat, how are you?"
3. "I am <u>fine</u>," Bob wrote.
4. "<u>Yesterday</u> I went to the park."
5. He signed it, "<u>Love</u>, Bob."
6. He will mail it <u>soon</u>.

Page 111
1. I can <u>hear</u> the dog bark.
2. I can hear with my <u>ear</u>.
3. I have two <u>eyes</u>.
4. I can see my <u>face</u> in the mirror.
5. My hat is on my <u>head</u>.
6. A <u>hand</u> has five fingers.

Answer Key

Page 113
May I say this?
He likes to run fast.
She had to look for him.
Can she buy a pencil?

Page 114
A rock is under a tree.
I will leave the car.
Please close the door.
Let's get another pumpkin.

Page 115
That plane can fly fast.
My dad eats the most.
A hand has five fingers.
I will write a letter to you.

Page 116
He hit a home run.
I will write a letter soon.
I can see with my eyes.
It goes right here.